SkySpirit

THE AMERICAN BALD EAGLE

SkySpirit

THE AMERICAN BALD EAGLE

MICHAEL FURTMAN

PHOTOGRAPHY BY
TOM AND PAT LEESON

NorthWord
PRESS, INC
MINOCQUA, WI 54548

NorthWord Press, Inc.
P.O. Box 1360
Minocqua, WI 54548

Cover design by Russell S. Kuepper
Book design and illustrations by Robin A. Pagel

Printed and bound in Canada

Library of Congress Cataloging-in-Publication Data

Furtman, Michael.
Sky spirit : the American bald eagle / by Michael Furtman ;
photography by Tom and Pat Leeson.
     p.   cm.
ISBN 1-55971-428-X (hardcover) : $29.95. — ISBN 1-55971-429-8
(softcover) : $19.95
1. Bald eagle. 2. Bald eagle—Pictorial works. I. Title.
QL696.F32F87   1994
598.9'16—dc20   94-20644
                              CIP

DEDICATION

In memory of my father Ralph Furtman

and his eagle-like parental devotion;

exemplary teacher, fierce defender,

diligent provider. May he soar unfettered

in the heaven of his dreams.

TABLE OF CONTENTS

PHOTOGRAPHERS' ACKNOWLEDGMENTS

In any major book project there are a great number of people who assist and help and who deserve credit.

A few of those whom we would like to thank include Jean Keene, an Alaskan whose commitment and dedication to eagles is as practical as it is inspirational. From December to April every year she devotes five to six hours a day, often in freezing temperatures, doing back-breaking work enabling hundreds of eagles to survive through the winter. Thanks, Jean, for helping the birds and for giving us the opportunity for many of the photos in this book.

We would like to express our appreciation to Tom Kitchin and Lynn Stone for the company, encouragement and general photographer camaraderie they have offered over the years on many an eagle photo trip. We'd also like to acknowledge fellow photographer Gary Vestal and the valuable insights and late night photo critiques he offered; but, mostly, we'll remember the gallons of premier strawberry ice cream he provided.

Our thanks to Dennis and Esther Schmidt for the assistance they provided years ago in helping us locate our first eagle nest. This proved the first step in what has become a fascinating adventure with eagles.

Thanks also to N.W. Trek and head keeper, Ed Cleveland, for allowing us to photograph eagle feathers in their possession.

Our hearts are always filled with gratitude to our parents who instilled a love of nature, and who taught us to work hard; and to our children, Laura and Sarah, who put up with hours of Mom and Dad being away photographing eagles.

Finally, we'd like to thank Kathleen Akerley who keeps our office running. Without her help captioning, labeling, and mailing, this book would have never happened.

INTRODUCTION

THE EAGLE'S WORLD

The bald eagle stood midstream, with the cold autumn waters rushing over its talons and the salmon they held. The young bird, its brown head streaked with white, bent to tear free and gulp down long strips of flesh.

Around the eagle other salmon swam and died, the end of their journey up this coastal river also the end of their lives. Spent spawners sank to the cobble bottom, rotting corpses nurturing myriad creatures in this stream. The tails and fins of salmon still spewing their reproductive worth broke the water's surface as they worked in the gravelly shallows. Eying these but content with its catch, the eagle ate voraciously, banking the ounces of fat needed to survive the winter, its crop filling when its stomach could hold no more.

Many other bald eagles fed or perched nearby— white-headed adults obvious, brown juveniles needing and benefiting by their camouflage. The chittering laughter of eagles pierced the cool air, and the screeched banter of two eagles squabbling over the same salmon rose above the sweet sound of mingling waters. Above the rapid water the river banks grew lushly green, defying the encroaching winter. Already a brush of high altitude snow lay upon the peaks of the brooding mountains that rose to the north and east.

Huge grizzly bears with rolls of fat rippling beneath thick cocoa fur strode down the green banks, crossed the cobbled beaches, and waded with grace and power into the fierce current. One bear leisurely dipped its broad head beneath the water, and scanned left and right, its shoulders and rump a woolly island. After what seemed an inordinately long time to hold one's breath, it burst up from below with yet another wriggling salmon squeezed in massive jaws. Eating the fatty parts and delicate roe, the bear tossed the remains aside and resumed its fishing.

As the young eagle stood on its catch, a sow grizzly led twin cubs past it up the shore. To the sow and first cub the eagle seemed not to exist, but the last cub turned toward the bird, stood half erect, and wondered at what it saw. The eagle nonchalantly fed, aware of, but not frightened by, the little bear. Huffing, the curious cub took two steps toward the eagle, and then with the distraction of youth, thought better and turned to race through the shallows after its mother and sibling. The eagle never flinched.

Together the river, the salmon, the bears, and the eagles prepared for winter, continuing the process in which death becomes life. This unending cycle with each creature a partner with a role unchanged in millennia, each partaking in a process inherently bloody and beautiful, intricate and fluid, played out along the river on this day.

The juvenile bald eagle knew little of this. For it the salmon were here not to spawn or feed bears, but brought bright from the dark sea so that eagles might live. The tall trees leaning from the river banks towered not so that they might bear cones and flourish, but so that eagles could perch and watch for the pulsing runs of fish. And for the eagle the sun rose to provide light for fishing, and to heat the earth so that eagles might ride the warm, rising winds. These things the eagle knew. These things all eagles know, and have known for millions of years.

Thorough is the eagle's knowledge of its world.

When we consider the lives of animals, we often do them a great injustice. Because we assume that animals don't learn in the same manner as we do, we also assume that they possess little knowledge, and that instinct governs all.

Instinct may be knowledge, knowledge learned over generations and passed through some molecular, chemical code. But beyond that speculation, animals that live long lives, such as the bald eagle, do learn. Instinct controls only part of their behavior; survival often depends upon lessons learned over the course of years.

In this book is much of what we know about the bald eagle. Our knowledge of them has recently become considerable. Mostly our research has come as a response to diminished numbers of these great birds, research mandated and funded by the noble and altruistic Endangered Species Act. It is only a shame that it took such a crisis to prompt our interest.

What we have learned is amazing, and garnered only after long hours afield by those who have dedicated years of their lives to this study. To these people we owe great thanks. Though many of us would imagine that such work is fun and rewarding (which it is), we forget the days and months these people spend away from family and the comforts of home, the tedious time spent in a cold, cramped blind, the risky climbs to the eagle's lofty nest, and the torment of black flies and mosquitoes in season.

Our new knowledge has served to help the bald eagle to reclaim its place in locations where we were responsible for its extirpation. And all that we learned the eagle already knew.

Like the eagle that ignored the gorging grizzlies as they shared the wealth of spawning salmon, it remains aloof from us. It doesn't much care what we do, so long as it can pursue what eagles have done and will always do. There is nothing that we know that is of use to the bald eagle, except what we have learned about giving these birds their due.

Who among us has not marveled at the dark form of a soaring eagle, and has wished that it were us above, able to traverse miles with eyes and wings? All that we have learned about this *spirit of the wind* has served to enhance that wonder. Considering their perfection of form, their stunning beauty, and their inspiring abilities, we are in their debt for the richness they bring to our lives.

CHAPTER ONE

FROM THE MISTS OF TIME

. . . .

Heat on the ocean rippled in illusionary waves, while the transparent waters beneath swelled as they eased toward the white sand shores. In a grand tree near the water's edge a large bird perched, scanning the shimmering waters for signs of life.

Flashing just beneath the water, a silver school of fish furrowed the surface as they skimmed along. The bird's yellow eyes intently followed the school, tension building in its rakish talons. As the fish occasionally bubbled in a cauldron of activity, breaking the water's surface, they were unaware that great wings were propelling the bird toward them. In a silent glide the eagle drifted over the fish, waiting for them to surface once more. As they skittered to the surface with a sound like rain on water, the talons of the plummeting eagle ripped through the school, lifting one fish into the air and carrying it to its death.

On a bare branch in the grand tree the eagle landed, folding its dark wings around its stout body, as one talon-tipped leg pinned the gasping fish to the wood. The flashing school of fish continued down the sandy shore, moving as if guided by a single thought, unaware of their loss. The eagle bent with scimitar bill to tear at its catch.

THE EVOLUTION OF
SEA EAGLES

Over 20 million years ago when the first sea eagle evolved somewhere along the Asian coast of the south Pacific, something like this fanciful scene surely took place. In this region and time the evolutionary history of sea eagles began, but not the evolution of predatory birds. For though this may have been the first sea eagle, it, too, had evolved from yet other birds of prey, most likely from the race of kites, to which today's eagles are still related.

The race of eagles is far more ancient than the race of man. 25 million years ago, when this progenitor of the bald eagle was already formed into what we would likely recognize as an eagle, apes in Africa had still another 15 million years of evolution to undergo before one species would evolve bipedal locomotion. And our family tree wouldn't begin to sprout from the evolutionary leap of that upright primate for yet another five million years. Still nearly another 4.9 million years would pass before someone we could call a truly human being could lift her eyes upward to watch the soaring of an eagle, this most ancient race.

It is very likely that those early humans marveled at the graceful flight of an eagle in much the same manner as we do today. Perhaps a bit of that ancient human lingers in us still, and helps us to form a sense of empathy and wonder at the grace and power of a fellow predator.

As we view this world from an egocentric vantage point that considers its wealth as ours to exploit, it is important that we consider how many races of creatures are more ancient than we, races whose form, could we travel back into our pre-history, we would recognize. If we could venture back in time and see this progenitor, we would know it, know by the way it rode the thermals, know by how it hunted and fed, that it was an eagle. That eagles predate us by such a monumental span surely gives us pause to wonder at how early and perfectly their evolution carried them to the niche they still fill.

Fossil records dating back 25 million years tell us of that first sea eagle. From this southeast Asian bird evolved all sea eagles, and adaptations continued until today we recognize eight sea and fish eagle species, of which our bald eagle is one.

RELATIVES OF THE
BALD EAGLE

These closely related sea and fish eagles inhabit all continents but Antarctica and South America. The bald eagle represents these eagles in North America. From the western shores of Greenland, through Iceland, Europe and east to Siberia soars the white-tailed sea eagle. Joining it along the Siberian coast and ranging south into Manchuria flies the Steller's sea eagle. Across the reaches of China lives the Pallas' sea eagle, and in that south-east region of Asia where the progenitor sea eagle evolved, as well as along the coasts of Australia, now lives the white-bellied sea eagle. Only in the Solomon Islands north of Australia does the Sanford's sea eagle live. West in Africa dwells the African fish eagle, and off that continent's coast lives the Madagascar fish eagle on that large island of the same name.

The Steller's sea eagle, named after Georg Wilhelm Steller, who in 1741 discovered the Aleutian Islands with Vitus Bering, is the giant among these birds. Known to weigh as much as 19 pounds, this bird of the seacoasts of northeast Asia is particularly handsome. This spectacular eagle has a massive bright yellow bill, and the white plumage on its tail, thighs, shoulders and forehead contrasts against a dark body and wings. Though primarily an eagle of Asia, the Steller's sea eagle sometimes wanders to the Pribilof Islands and coast of Alaska where it joins the company of bald eagles.

Inhabiting the same latitudes across Europe and Asia as our own bald eagle does across North America, the white-tailed sea eagle is the bald eagle's nearest relative. Though it lacks the white head of the bald eagle, its white tail is every bit as brilliant as that of the bald eagle.

One of the smallest of this group, the African fish eagle is a handsome bird ranging throughout the southern two thirds of that continent. Observers describe the call of this particularly vocal eagle as melodious yodeling. Black wings and a brown belly set off the flashy white tail, and the white of the head and neck flows lower onto the shoulders than it does on the bald eagle. The related African and Madagascar fish eagles are particularly skilled at catching live fish. The Madagascar fish eagle shares the African fish eagle's white tail, though its head is grayish.

A primarily brown eagle, the Pallas sea eagle lives near inland waters of central Asia where it feeds often on dead or dying fish and other carrion. About the same size as the bald eagle, the Pallas' sea eagle shares the characteristic of gathering in large numbers during the winter months.

Almost as big as the bald eagle is the white-bellied sea eagle of coastal southern Asia and Australia. It is a grayish brown and white eagle, with the white portions brilliant on the underbelly, neck and head. Its close cousin, the Sanford's sea eagle of the Solomon Islands lacks the white markings that are so typical of the other fish and sea eagles.

No one knows why no sea eagles inhabit South America. Some scientists speculate that they simply have not yet reached that continent as they have evolved and spread across the globe from their evolutionary homeland of southeast Asia. Perhaps the bald eagle of North America would have eventually pioneered its way south to fill this niche had not their numbers been so reduced in modern times. Given the long tides on which evolution floats, perhaps someday they will yet expand south.

SHARED BEHAVIORS

That most ancient progenitor eagle of southeast Asia likely evolved from kites, a fork-tailed hunting and scavenging bird of the genus Haliastur. When this evolutionary step took place still is unclear, but we do know through fossil records that this ancient sea eagle existed 25 million years ago. Even today, all sea and fish eagles continue to share common traits with their kite relations, including courtship and breeding habits, and the manner in which they scavenge, steal and hunt for food.

Many other predatory birds share some or all of these characteristics, for kites are not the sea eagle's only close relations. The Order Falconiformes consists of five families. One of these families, Accipitridae, includes the bald eagle and 205 species of Old World vultures, kites, harriers, hawks and other eagles. More specifically, the bald eagle is within the genus Haliaeetus, which also includes the other seven sea and fish eagles already named. Indeed, there are some 298 worldwide species within this order. Approximately 60 species are called eagles, although that title is less than specific. Just what makes a bird of prey an eagle and not a hawk is not taxonomically standardized, and some birds receive their eagle status rather randomly.

With the owls, which are not a member of the Order Falconiformes, these birds are commonly referred to as birds of prey. Owls differ from other birds of prey in that the top of their bill lacks the fleshy cere through which the nostrils open. They also have soft feathers that allow them to fly more silently than most all other birds of prey whose stiffer primaries are noisier in flight.

As carnivores, they are enviously well equipped for their role, and they are all, to one degree or another, either expert scavengers, expert hunters, or both. Completely reliant upon insects, meat, or innards for their diets, birds of prey possess sharp, curved bills for the tearing of flesh, and muscular feet equipped with scythe-like talons featuring opposable hind toes for capturing and gripping their prey.

A less formally recognized classification between the level of genus and species is called "superspecies."

The bald eagle and its sea and fish eagle relatives are members of three superspecies groups that denotes the nearest possible relationship before interbreeding occurs. For instance, the two subspecies of bald eagle, Haliaeetus leucocephalus leucocephalus (the southern race) and Haliaeetus leucocephalus alascanus (the northern race) are perfectly capable of breeding together. In fact, they are really only distinguished by their breeding areas and that the northern subspecies tend to be larger than southern bald eagles. These then are members of the same species.

Members of a superspecies would include the bald eagle and its close cousin, the white-tailed sea eagle, which occupies similar latitudes and habitats across the Old World. Other superspecies within the sea and fish eagle group includes the linking of the African and Madagascar fish eagles, as well as the pairing of the Sanford's and white-bellied sea eagles.

All these eagles share the common trait of dwelling near water, and though some may wear the title sea eagle, they may never see a sea. Inland lakes and rivers provide suitable habitats for many of these species, and the Pallas' sea eagle of central Asia actually is never found on any sea coast. But, among the common characteristics of these eagles is their diet of fish, though most will also occasionally prey on small mammals or scavenge upon larger ones. The white-bellied sea eagle regularly includes sea snakes in its diet, while the Sanford's eagle is thought to hunt birds and mammals in that portion of its inland mountain range.

EAGLES AND PEOPLE

Like the bald eagle, whose numbers dropped dramatically beginning with European settlement of North America and culminated in near extinction across much of its range by the 1970s, the related seven species of fish and sea eagles numbers have dwindled to varying degrees. The Madagascar fish eagle faces extinction in its limited range. The white-tailed eagle, found in healthy numbers across much of its vast territory, has suffered local extinctions in Britain and Europe. From outright persecution by the ignorant, to insidious food chain poisoning by industrial and agricultural toxins, every sea and fish eagle species has sustained losses in all or part of their ranges. And as serious as each of these causes are, in many places eagles no longer exist for neither of these reasons, but simply because there are too many of us. Habitat loss looms as the ultimate threat.

That we have caused so much harm to eagles worldwide seems on the surface a strange thing considering our admiration for them. Nearly every society of humans has at some time been enamored of these great birds, though in few places has this appreciation reached the level of respect and reverence that it did in North America. Virtually every Native American tribe considered bald and golden eagles to be special emissaries of the Creator.

Europeans, whose descendants persecuted both the bald eagle and the Native Americans upon landing in North America, also once held respect for the eagle. As a national symbol, the eagle has graced the staffs, battle flags and tapestries of Russia, Turkey, Austria and Poland. In addition as the popularity of falconry spread during the Middle Ages, the distinction of owning and hunting with eagles was reserved for emperors.

Because it was associated with Zeus, the Roman legions two thousand years ago adopted the eagle as their ensign. The ancient Egyptians' funeral rights included the release of eagles, on whose wings the spirits of the deceased were born to the after-life.

All of which is a lot to foist upon a bird whose ancestry is far older than those who have admired it, and that neither understands, nor cares about, our emblematic or spiritual fancies. Still, our fascination with these great birds is understandable. Of all the human predilections toward other creatures, envy of flight may have been the first. Who among us has not stopped to wonder how it is that these mighty birds soar so easily? How often have members of our race dreamed of possessing that ability? How logical then that as we toiled earthbound we stood in awe of these mighty birds effortlessly floating above and saw in them the spirit of the wind.

That the eagle, who flies so high and displays such fearsome strength and skill in the hunt, should immediately hold our fancy shouldn't be surprising. To an aspiring race of two-legged hunters tentatively spreading across a virgin planet, an admiration for such an obviously skilled fellow hunter would only seem logical.

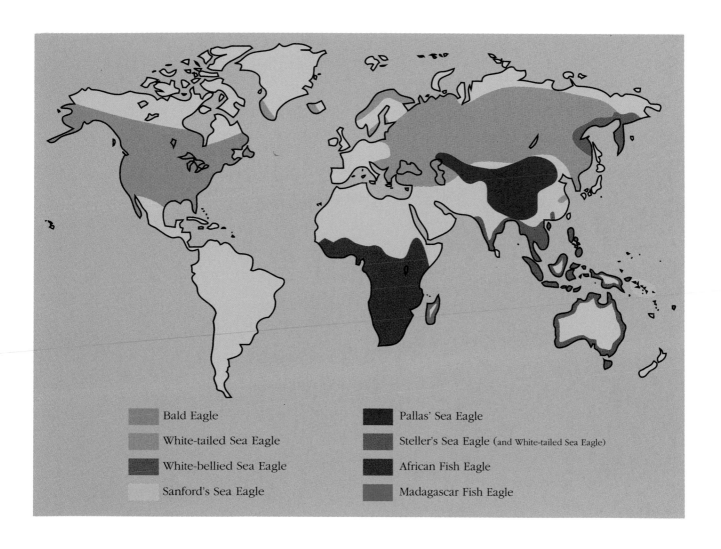

	Bald Eagle		Pallas' Sea Eagle
	White-tailed Sea Eagle		Steller's Sea Eagle (and White-tailed Sea Eagle)
	White-bellied Sea Eagle		African Fish Eagle
	Sanford's Sea Eagle		Madagascar Fish Eagle

CHAPTER TWO

MI-GE-ZI—THE BALD EAGLE

Long ago, when the earth was new, everything was going well according to the universal harmony that the Great Spirit set in motion.

Then the Anishinabe did some disrespectful things, so the Creator sent a warning that the people would be destroyed. The bald eagle, a close friend of Anishinabeg, heard the news and volunteered to fly to the Creator's world. This took much bravery, as the bird would have to fly close to the sun and could be destroyed by the heat.

So, on a given day, the eagle announced his departure and flew up, up and away toward the sun. Soon the bird was just a speck in the sky. The eagle flew around the sun, onward toward the Creator. Finally it landed in the Creator's world.

"Who is walking in my world?" boomed the Creator. "It is I, Mi-Ge-Zi," the Eagle said in a trembling voice.

"What is it you wish?" the Creator asked.

"I have come because I love Anishinabeg and I ask that you consider something besides destroying them. Perhaps you could send teachers to instruct them about the good life. Perhaps these teachers could teach about the old ways of respect and honor among all creatures large and small."

"You speak bravely and with great wisdom. Yes, I will send teachers. They will be called Elders. Some will be messengers; others will be teachers who have lived long, respectful lives. These will be the ones who have gained experience, the ones who live in harmony with all creatures and all earthly beings; the ones who tell the stories, the ones who remember the old ways when all creatures and beings lived and worked together like in the beginning."

"Mi-Ge-Zi, Eagle, you are a brave and courageous being. For your strong character and heroic act on behalf of Anishinabeg, from this day forth, everything that is yours will be honored and revered as sacred. Your image, your feathers, your claws will be as symbols and messages of connections and communications to my world. From now on, all those who respect and honor you will get special help from me. Those who your symbols protect, I will protect. Those who seek refuge in your power will bear my message to all beings on Earth."

"Go back then and remain with Anishinabeg. You will also be a messenger, a teacher, a symbol of courage and strength, respect, sacredness and honor."

That is why people must respect and honor the eagle.

(Legend as told by Jimmy Jackson, Anishinabe Medicine Man. From the pamphlet *Bald Eagles,* edited and compiled by John Mathisen, Biologist, Chippewa National Forest, USDA Forest Service publication.)

EMISSARY TO THE CREATOR

To the Anishinabe people of my home state of Minnesota, who are also known as Chippewa or Ojibwa, the bald eagle is among the most revered of all creatures, an understandable status considering its intercession against destruction. For them, there was no question of what the bald eagle was, or how it fit in the scheme of things. It was a fellow hunter, a different race, and a creature to be respected. Because of the bald eagle's ties with the Creator, the Anishinabe believed that it was one of the Spirit Keepers of the Four Directions; Wabun of the East.

Reverence for the bald, and golden, eagle is almost universal among Native Americans, and it stands in striking contrast to the attitudes of the European immigrants to this continent. Some tribes held the belief that a person holding an eagle feather could not tell a lie. When eagle feathers were attached to a peace pipe they added increased importance to an object already sacred to nearly all Indian cultures. If the feathers were attached to

the mouthpiece, no impure words could be spoken as the pipe was smoked. An eagle feather tied near the union of the bowl and stem sped the healing of wounds of body or soul.

Shamans used eagle feathers in their mystic practice. Hopi shamans laid a puhu, or road, of eagle feathers from the grave of the departed, guiding the soul to the west, the direction of the underworld. A similar puhu was laid to show disease a path from the village.

Eagle feathers had particular meaning to warrior cultures. The Cherokee taught that only approved warriors dared wear an eagle feather, and the Creek war flag was made of eagle feathers. Shields painted with the image of an eagle, or decorated with its feathers, were believed to give the bearer the swiftness and courage of this admired bird.

Lakota warriors attached great meaning to the color and location of eagle feathers worn in their hair. If a warrior counted coup (struck an enemy on the battlefield with a ritual stick) he was allowed to wear an eagle feather upright in his scalp lock. This non-lethal method of warfare evolved among the plains Indians to minimize bloodshed between rival tribes while still allowing displays of bravery and protection of territorial boundaries. If a warrior was wounded, he was entitled to wear upright an eagle feather with quill dyed red. A warrior who successfully took horses from an enemy could wear a green quilled eagle feather suspended from his scalp lock. Warriors who had escaped an enemy wore a suspended yellow eagle feather. By observing the color and position of a warrior's eagle feathers, his status and accomplishments could be instantly assessed.

The Pueblos believed eagles were related to the sun. They performed the sacred Eagle Dance as part of a ritual cure for illness and to promote health. Dressed as, and performing the roles of, a male and female eagle, the dancers depicted eagle behaviors. Swooping to earth signified the gathering of human prayers.

Eagle dances performed for a variety of reasons were part of the culture of the Choctaw, Iroquois, Iowa and Cherokee peoples. Membership in the Iroquois Confederacy, whose symbol was the bald eagle, was indicated by the wearing of an eagle feather. Indians of the Pacific Northwest honored the eagle in many realistic totem carvings, often placing them at the top of these poles as messengers to the spirit world.

Compare this reverence to the attitude of a great American, no less than Benjamin Franklin, who, in a 1784 letter to his daughter, derided the choice of the bald eagle as his country's emblem:

"For my part, I wish that the bald eagle had not been chosen as the representative of our country; he is a bird of bad moral character; he does not get his living honestly; you may see him perched on some dead tree, where, too lazy to fish for himself, he watches the labor of the fishing-hawk; when that diligent bird has at length taken a fish, and is bearing it to his nest for the support of his mate and young ones, the bald eagle pursues him and takes it from him."

One could probably write a thesis on the way two cultures view the same bird, with each culture coming to

such a contrasting conclusion based on the same evidence. Native Americans knew this bird and its habits well. They saw the bald eagle's tendency to feed on carrion. Yet they did not judge this bird as cowardly, lazy, or brand it a thief, but saw instead an emissary to the Creator, one whose eating habits did little to diminish its spiritual stature.

Europeans, by contrast, had begun their persecution of eagles on their home continent, spurred on by the mistaken impression that eagles kill livestock. Like the wolf that is subject to so many morbid fairy tales, the eagle was believed to attack humans. Old wives' tales brought to this continent told of eagles that would swoop down to carry away babies.

There is little advantage in judging the relative merits of differing cultures. However, in this case, it would be much easier to prove Franklin wrong since the eagle's eating habits have nothing to do with morality.

A NICHE OF ITS OWN

The bald eagle's value is not based upon our assessments of it anyway. It has a role independent of our perspective, a niche filled for millions of years.

Still, as we struggle to learn more about the natural world around us, scientists seek ways to define species in an objective manner. From our study of the bald eagle we have learned that its evolutionary history is long and its adaptations for survival are intricate.

Though we do not know when one expanding race of eagles became the bald eagle, we do know that this bird is a relative newcomer to North America. Fossil remains here date back

about one million years. The tar pits of California have yielded many eagle bones, as have sites in South Dakota, Alaska and a dozen other states. This date is not definitive. It represents only the earliest known bald eagle fossils, not their arrival here. The evidence does show that the bald eagle has been playing its role on the seacoasts, lakes and rivers of North America much longer than have humans. Nor should we view its evolution as static, as something that has stopped. It is likely that changes are still occurring within the race of bald eagles, and what we know about it now is merely a single frame taken from an eons-long film.

PREDATOR AND SCAVENGER

What we do know of the bald eagle as it exists today can be quantified and measured. The bald eagle is an apex predator; a creature at the top of the food chain, much as we are. It is a large diurnal raptor; a bird of prey that hunts by day. Of the eight sea eagles, the bald eagle is among the largest and can weigh up to 14 pounds. Wings can span seven and a half feet; in North America, only the California condor and the golden eagle are larger.

Predators are an interesting lot; creatures that have evolved to feed upon others. Because the bald eagle often feeds upon dead fish or mammal carrion, it seemingly crosses the line of scavenging. In reality, just about all predators are at least part-time scavengers, opportunistically taking advantage of food that they did not kill. Wolves, which historically occupied much of the same North American

territory as did bald eagles, also take advantage of carrion, though they, too, are predators of the first rank. Wolves and eagles have even been known to scavenge at the same carcass. Even humans, when purchasing a pound of hamburger at the market, are effectively acting as a scavenger, since they did not kill the cow.

Predation and scavenging take advantage of the most highly concentrated food source: meat. The caloric value of meat by volume is far greater than that of any plant source. Although I've not seen any studies comparing the time budget of feeding bald eagles with similarly sized grazing birds, such as geese or turkeys, it is very likely that the eagle would spend less time hunting and feeding than geese would spend grazing. Scavenging allows the eagle to feed on mammals far too large for it to kill, a versatility that increases its odds of survival.

Predation and scavenging probably result in a time advantage for the bald eagle; part of that time is spent in devotion to its young, a task that requires enormous energy by both members of a mated pair.

Like many other scavenging predators, bald eagles spend much of their long life (captive bald eagles have lived to 47; wild birds probably rarely survive past 30 years) in small groups. Compare this to grazing geese again, whose flock size can number in the thousands. Though eagles sometimes gather in groups during the winter when food is concentrated, even these groups are not large compared to grazing birds, and most of an eagle's life will be spent in the company of its mate, and a particular year's offspring. Most bald eagle researchers conclude that mated bald eagles form long monogamous bonds, but they replace mates very quickly (often within days) when one dies.

MORE THAN JUST A WHITE HEAD

The bald eagle's formal name is Haliaeetus leucocephalus (which means "sea eagle with a white head"). There are two subspecies of the bald eagle: Haliaeetus leucocephalus leucocephalus, the southern race; and Haliaeetus leucocephalus alascanus, the northern race. The two subspecies are differentiated only by their size, and the boundary between the two subspecies has been arbitrarily set at 40 degrees north latitude.

The bald eagle has alternately been known as the white-headed eagle, white-headed sea eagle, and the American eagle before the "bald" name took hold. Of course, the bird isn't bald; the appellation is rooted in the French word "blanc," which means white. In archaic English "blanc" became "balde." It has been applied not only to the bald eagle, but also to the wigeon duck, which is sometimes called "bald pate" ("pate" is an antiquated word referring to the top of the head).

Although alike in color, female bald eagles are larger than the males, which is a common characteristic among raptors. In proportion to the rest of her body, the female bald eagle's bill and feet are larger than those of the male. Body length for adults and juveniles of both sexes and both subspecies is from 28 to 38 inches. Wingspread varies from a low of 66 inches to a high of 96. Weights range

from 6 1/2 to 14 pounds.

Northern bald eagles are so much larger than their southern counterparts, that northern males are larger than southern females. This large body adaptation is known as Bergmann's Rule and applies to many other warm-blooded species of birds and animals that inhabit widely disparate habitats. In the north, large bodies are an advantage because they lose heat at a slower rate. In the mid-latitude states where the two bald eagle subspecies meet, it is difficult to distinguish between the two, as the size difference is miminal.

THE EYES HAVE IT— TOOLS OF THE PREDATOR

Legends of the eagle's exceptional eyesight are largely true. Sight is the bald eagle's most important sense, and it is thought that their distance vision exceeds ours fourfold. The eyes consume most of the space in a bald eagle's head and are almost as large as human eyes. Bald eagle eyes are imposing, and range in color from buff to bright yellow. Rod and cone cells that gather light and color fill the eye's large retina. Most of the eagle's retina is given over to cones for increased acuity and color perception. In low light conditions, color differentiation diminishes. The rods take over and the eagle sees objects in varying shades of gray. With fewer rods than cones, the bald eagle's night vision is not especially refined, which is reflected in this bird's proclivity to hunt by day.

While the human retina contains one depression called a fovea, the bald eagle's contains two, creating vision that is both sharper and more powerful than ours. One fovea faces forward while the other is directed sideways, further enhancing vision. Protecting these remarkable eyes are eyelids similar to ours, as well as a transparent membrane that sweeps sideways every three or four seconds to keep the eye clean and moist.

Their eyes face forward, giving the bald eagle binocular vision similar to humans. Binocular vision allows for precise depth of field, which is important for humans manipulating small objects with our hands, or for eagles that must snatch prey with talons while diving from the sky. Unlike our eyes, the eagle's eyes are, in addition, partially autonomous, allowing independent monocular vision to the sides. Thus, they have better peripheral vision than you and I. Able to move their eyes only slightly within the sockets, eagles instead rotate their head to see.

Apparently, the sense of smell is not very important to bald eagles, although they do possess good hearing and a voice. Eagle communication takes advantage of their excellent vision—they soar to mark territory and posture to defend themselves, their young, or food—but they also communicate by voice. Bald eagle pairs greet each other upon arrival at the nest, and females appear to let males know they are willing to copulate with a soft, high, solicitation call. The downy eaglets are particularly vocal when demanding to be fed. Bald eagles will also give voice when facing intruders and to stake claims to food or preferred roosting sites.

One can hardly look at a portrait of a bald eagle without noticing, and being impressed by, their imposing bill. The bald eagle's curved, yellow

beak is almost three inches long and is primarily used as a tool to tear at flesh. However, when the eagle is so inclined, or the prey is small, it is used as a weapon. Eagles do not chew food, but swallow it in chunks, and the bill can be opened quite wide to accommodate this task.

Guided by its incredible eyesight, the bald eagle's primary weapons are its powerful talons. Much as we are able to clench our hand, the bald eagle's three forward and one rear toes can close securely. Each toe is tipped with a blackish-gray, two-inch talon that is sharp enough to puncture prey and can be locked to secure the struggling meal. Its legs are long, powerful and feathered except the lower portions and feet, which are covered in a scaly yellow skin. The undersides of the toes are covered in fleshy knobs that probably aid in gripping both prey and perches.

SIZE, SHAPE AND PLUMAGE

The adult bald eagle of both sexes has the brilliant white head for which it is named, as well as a white tail, which is comprised of 12 feathers measuring from 11 to 16 inches in length. The tail is rounded in shape (as opposed to the wedge shape of the closely related white-tailed sea eagle) and can be spread out in flight to provide control. The remaining feathers are predominantly dark brown rimmed in lighter brown. Some evidence indicates that southern bald eagles are lighter in color than northern birds. On rare occasions blond and albino bald eagles have been observed.

Attaining adult plumage occurs gradually as juvenile birds go through a succession of molts. Dark brown in its first year, by the third year streaks of white appear on the head and tail of subadult bald eagles. With each year and molt, more white is added. By their fourth summer most birds develop their white head and tail, though it is grayish and less brilliant than in an adult.

Bald eagles molt once a year, though this feather rejuvenating process may last up to six months. Nesting adults begin their molt while they are incubating their eggs. Nonbreeding eagles start molting earlier and complete it faster. Though eventually all feathers are replaced, not all feathers are replaced each year. Bald eagles retain feathers on portions of the wing through some molt cycles so that it can always fly. Molting begins at the head and works down the body until the tail feather molt begins in July or August. By autumn, the molt is complete.

Juvenile bald eagles are actually a different shape from the adults, and as they grow older and molt, their tail shortens and their wings get narrower. Because of their broader, longer wings, young bald eagles enjoy less mass and greater wing area, causing them to soar more easily than adults. This may be an adaptation to allow them to search more effortlessly for the carrion on which they depend until they perfect their hunting skills.

Generally, the wings of a bald eagle are wide and long, characteristic of a large soaring raptor. Females have longer wings than males, and in both sexes the large wings can make landing and take-off difficult for young

birds. Because of their weight distribution, bald eagles are preeminent gliders—they are capable of soaring for hours with barely a flap of their wings. Soaring, however, would be impossible without the warm upwelling air currents known as thermals and other air currents, such as those created along shorelines, river valleys and the face of ridges. Eagles evolved into expert soarers to reduce the energy needed to flap their enormous wings, a trait especially important for long distance travel.

At the tip of each wing are the finger-like feathers known as primaries; they can be adjusted individually to reduce turbulence or to enhance stability and maneuverability. Mid-wing are the secondary feathers that comprise the most surface area. Supporting the wing is the humerus, a long bone that is hollow to reduce weight. Evolution has created a durable skeleton that actually weighs less than do all the feathers.

These combined features allow the eagle to be remarkably agile for a bird of its size. Except for juveniles, which are awkward fliers at first, bald eagles can perform incredible aerobatics. They have been known to turn upside down while snatching food from the talons of an osprey, or to outmaneuver a swift flying duck that is destined to become eagle food.

ON THE WING— WHAT BIRD IS THAT?

Existing in a brown phase for over three years, juvenile bald eagles can be mistaken for other large soaring birds. Even adults with their distinctive plumage can be difficult to identify when drifting overhead, especially when at a distance or back-lit by the sun. People sometimes misidentify bald eagles as ospreys (a large, fish eating hawk that shares much of the bald eagle's range), turkey vultures, and golden eagles (the only other eagle native to North America). Observation provides clues to identification. Pay particular attention to wing position while the bird soars, body proportions, and the location of any white, or light, patches on the wings or undersides.

Ospreys are smaller than bald eagles and glide with their wings in a dihedral shape; wings appearing slightly bent. They also exhibit much white on the underside of the head, breast and the leading portions of the first half of their wings.

Turkey vultures, also smaller than a bald eagle, appear to have less head and more tail than the bald eagle when seen from below. From below, vulture wings appear gray in back and black in front. Seen from ahead or behind, the wings of a vulture are held in a V shape while soaring and the entire bird tends to wobble in flight. Vultures are more likely than bald eagles to soar in groups, circling in a formation known as a kettle.

Immature bald eagles are often mistaken for golden eagles because of the similarities in size and coloration. Distinguishing between the two depends on telltale differences in plumage. The young bald eagle is often streaked with white under the body and wings, and on head and tail. No white shows on an adult golden eagle, and subadults will display small wedges of white only on the wings and at the base of the tail. If an eagle seen from below clearly shows white at the point where body and wing meet, it

can only be a juvenile bald eagle. Like the turkey vulture, a golden eagle appears to have less head forward of the body when observed from below.

The golden eagle is a member of the group of booted eagles in the genus Aquila. The legs of booted eagles are feathered to the toes. The lower leg of the bald eagle is bare. Despite their similarities in size, bald and golden eagles are really very different creatures. Golden eagles have different evolutionary roots, fill a different ecological niche, and are behaviorally distinct from bald eagles. Though they share North America with the bald eagle, they are also distributed across Eurasia, North Africa, the Middle East, southwestern China, Pakistan, India, Korea, and Japan. Generally associated with mountainous and desert terrain where they nest on cliffs and ride terrain-induced thermals, golden eagles feed primarily on small mammals. They are solitary hunters that rarely congregate, unlike the bald eagle that may gather in large numbers during the winter. In North America they inhabit parts of Mexico, the western United States, Alaska, and most of Canada. Though rare now in the eastern U.S., they also include the northern Appalachians in their territory.

RANGE AND STATUS

When Europeans arrived in North America, the bald eagle was found along both coasts, along every major river, throughout the Great Lakes region, and just about everywhere there was water to support their primarily fish diet. From Florida to Baja California, from Labrador to Alaska, the bald eagle reared its young in huge stick nests placed in tall trees at water's edge. Though no one knows exactly how many bald eagles existed then, some postulate they could have numbered approximately one-half million.

Reports from the mid-1800s tell of large numbers of bald eagles on the ice of the Hudson River near Manhattan Island, New York. Minnesota observers claimed every large lake had its pair of eagles. Bald eagles were abundant in the cypress swamps of the south. In 1890, the 5,620 miles of Chesapeake Bay shoreline was reported to have one nest per mile. Using computations based on recent research of nest occupancy rates and territory size, and factoring in non-breeding eagles, this region may have been home to as many as twelve thousand bald eagles!

However many existed in a more pristine North America, the settling of this continent was not kind to the bald eagle. Its population declined through shootings, poisoning, and habitat destruction. Pesticides, particularly DDT, caused a calamitous collapse of the eagle population only a few decades ago. More recently, the species that caused the bald eagle's near demise has also been responsible for aiding it in its remarkable comeback.

Responding to our efforts to protect it, bald eagle numbers have been steadily increasing over the past two decades. As recently as 1963, as few as 417 adult nesting pairs could be found in the lower 48 states. Efforts to decrease adult mortality, to reduce pollution that was poisoning or removing food sources, and to protect some nesting and wintering territories began to allow the bald eagle to use its

remarkable survival strategies to rebuild its population. By 1992 the number of adult bald eagles occupying nesting territories had increased to 3,747. Since juvenile bald eagles are not counted in these surveys, the actual number of eagles in the lower 48 is much higher than these numbers indicate.

Canada and Alaska have enjoyed similar increases in bald eagle numbers, and for the first time in decades, the status of bald eagles appears good. Only time will tell whether the trend will continue.

Comparison of the bald eagle with other similar species, flying and perched. This page, from top to bottom: turkey vulture, osprey, red-tailed hawk; facing, from top to bottom: immature bald eagle, adult bald eagle, immature golden eagle, adult golden eagle.

Illustrations by John F. McGee

CHAPTER THREE

HOME RANGE

*S*tartled from its perch the bald eagle flushed into the June sky, its powerful wings rowing to gain altitude. It swept along the birch and pine shoreline of the lake, landing in a snag-topped white pine, its white head a brilliant beacon as it folded its dark wings. Finding its balance on the narrow branch, the eagle turned to watch as a red canoe rounded the stony point behind which it had been feeding.

Paddling north through the long succession of linked bays that is Crooked Lake, a 26-mile-long, twisting body of water on the border of the Minnesota-Ontario wilderness, we reached a spot where the cold waters were squeezed between dark banks of slab granite. In such narrow spots between shorelines or islands, this majestic lake spawns strong currents, behaving much like a river. Increasing the tempo of our paddle strokes, we labored against the flow. A flash of movement and the stirring of air beneath wings alerted us to the departing, startled eagle.

As volunteer wilderness rangers for the United States Forest Service, my wife, Mary Jo, and I were touring our territory. While most of our duties were to check on campers or campsites, this day brought us to this spot specifically to watch for the eagles of Wednesday Bay, assisting in the monitoring of eagles in the

Boundary Waters Canoe Area Wilderness. Cold breezes drifted from the north through a wan blue sky, barely hinting at the summer to come, but typical of the tardy spring in the north. It was good fortune that we had found an eagle so easily.

This eagle, we believed, was one of a pair that nests on the Canadian shore of Wednesday Bay. It solemnly watched us as we turned our canoe from the current toward where it had been perched. At that spot a tall, dark pine leaned out over the water. Two thirds of the way up its stout trunk, in a fork of thick branches, was one of the pairs' three nests. This one was in disrepair, its straggle of sticks a nest by only a stretch of imagination. Obviously the nest had not been used in some time. Pale blue sky shined through the stacked sticks. As we neared we could see something large and pink washed up on shore beneath the tree. A current of air brought a sickening odor to us. Easing nearer we recognized a rotting, sorry carcass of a moose, its bloated form stripped of its dark hair so that it lay, pink and blue, like a grotesque beach ball. Large rents in the flesh were obvious signs of the eagle's powerful hooked bill.

Not that the eagle was in any way responsible for the death of this huge animal. This moose had died sometime during the subzero northern winter, and had succumbed for one reason or another while the eagles were far to the south. Though we could never know, it was a safe bet that the moose had broken through ice kept thin by the swirling currents below, drowning beneath its white surface.

That the carcass was largely intact bolstered that theory. Had it died on the surface it would have been consumed by the wolves and coyotes that live in the region, the skeleton left to sink when the May sun finally freed the region of ice. If wolves had been responsible for driving the moose out onto the treacherous ice, they obviously had not benefited by the accident. More likely the moose had simply chosen this narrow spot to cross to browse in the forest beyond.

We couldn't know how often such events occurred, but I had a feeling the eagles did. Any spot within their home range that would provide such a large bonanza of food upon their arrival certainly would be remembered. Such a protein feast after a long migration and during the critical egg laying

and incubation periods would be, in some years, a great aid in successfully rearing a brood.

While we speculated, the unperturbed eagle watched us. Not wanting to disrupt its feeding any longer, we turned away from the putrid carcass, paddling quietly off to search for the pair's active nest.

TERRITORY SHAPE AND SIZE

Within our "territory" as rangers, were the territories of three pairs of bald eagles. Like the eagles, our territory was one with which we were intimately familiar, but the similarities stopped there. We did not depend on our territory to supply food, except the occasional fish dinner or berries in season; our food was packed in. And we were not depending on the lushness or solitude of our territory to provide the resources necessary to raise any little rangers. We also had no need to defend our territory. Because our food came from elsewhere and we had no "fledglings," we lacked incentive to keep others from the area's resources.

But the eagles did. Since securing the resources of a particular area can be critical to their survival, bald eagles are highly territorial birds. For the sake of this discussion, a territory is that part of the landscape surrounding their nest site(s) that a pair feels compelled to defend. Eagle researchers also refer to a "home range," or that slightly larger area in which the eagles may frequently forage, and may even share with other mated pairs or non-breeding eagles. The home range is not vigorously defended, and is more elastic in shape than an eagle's territory.

Within a mated pair's breeding territory will be found their nest and perching and roosting sites, which only they can use. These territories are traditional, and pairs, which may mate for life, apparently return to the same territory each breeding season. The heart of their territory will be on the water's edge, with a suitable nesting tree at its core. Generally, the territory is longer (along the shore) than it is wide (back into the forest), since shorelines provide open views for defense, updrafts to aide soaring, and places to perch and hunt. Isolation reduces interference during nesting. Pairs protect this isolation through both aggressive and, more frequently, ritualized defense. Not only will the pair eject competing eagles, but they will defend eggs or nestlings from predators.

Territory size and shape is widely variable. It may include a cone-shaped air space above the nest. It may also extend farther out into the water than it does inland, presumably because visibility is greater over the water, and because water (with its fish) is more critical to their survival. Shoreline length may influence the number of eagles in an area. For instance, a large, irregularly shaped lake, one with many bays, islands, and points, might support more bald eagles than a linear body of water with less shoreline.

In some regions bald eagle territories are smaller than in others. One could speculate that this has much to do with the availability of food resources. Bald eagles nesting in areas with plentiful food supplies tend to nest nearer one another than in places where competition for scarce food would lead to poor reproduction. The more readily available food is, the greater the potential number of nesting pairs.

Generally, occupied bald eagle nests are no nearer to each other than about one-half mile, with the average distance being closer to one mile. Some very notable exceptions occur. Both in Florida and Alaska occupied nests have been observed as near to each other as 300 yards. Pairs that nest in more temperate climates may never stray far from their territories, while those that nest farther north migrate to and from their nesting territory each year.

Perching trees along the edge of a pair's territory may delineate boundaries as well as serve as sites from which to watch for food and intruders. Since a breeding territory must meet three important criteria (be near water/food, contain a suitable nest tree, and be vacant of other eagles), there is a finite number of bald eagles that can nest in a particular region.

Though the eagles may hunt within their breeding territory, much of their food gathering takes place within the larger home range. A pair may choose to defend or share this larger foraging area. Home ranges are more elastic than nesting territories and may well change with the wind direction, on which eagles are largely dependent for soaring, an important hunting tool.

DEFENSE

That bald eagles would evolve a territorial imperative isn't surprising. Most predators depend upon some level of territoriality. Because predators depend upon other creatures as a food source, and because there is a finite prey base, the ability to control an area in which you are the sole hunter and breeder (of your species), is a tremendous advantage. Life is tenuous enough without having to worry about competition by others of your kind for food or breeding habitat. The greater the amount of control that can be exercised, the less that is left to chance.

That advantage, though, comes with a set of problems inherent in "owning" a territory. In order to control it, one must be able to defend it. Fortunately for most predators, they have also evolved methods of defending a territory that reduces actual physical confrontation.

Like the wolf that howls to let others of their kind know where they are located, bald eagles also give vocal warnings to intruders. Think of this as a kind of auditory fence. The wolf also uses scent markings around the edge of its territory to delineate its boundaries. Since scent is not important to bald eagles, they use a visual means of marking the boundaries of their territory.

The bald eagle's version of the wolf's howl is a piercing, ringing territorial call. Tossing its head back, a defending eagle will declare its occupancy by first voicing a brief, loud grunt which is rapidly repeated three or four times and followed by the ringing territorial call; a loud, excited, high-pitched "whee-he-he-he" that has often

been described as resembling the neighing of a horse.

Though bald eagles don't scent mark their territorial boundaries as do wolves and some other mammalian predators, they have evolved a non-vocal means of marking their boundaries, taking advantage of their incredible eyesight. Mature bald eagles spend a considerable part of each day perched in prominent places around their territory. Their brilliant white heads and tails, which may have evolved partially to aid this process, serve as beacons readily seen by any other eagles passing near.

Adult bald eagles also spend much time soaring above their nest on days when conditions are favorable. From this height they can be seen for miles by other eagles, and researchers believe this conspicuous soaring may further demonstrate possesion of a territory.

These adaptations show possession of territory while minimizing effort, with the energy better spent on incubation or brood rearing. Visual and auditory defense also aids in avoiding physical conflict. Inherent in actual physical confrontation is the risk of injury. Avoiding confrontation and possible injury is therefore to the advantage of both the intruder and the defender.

Not that it always works that way. Bald eagles do, on occasion, physically defend their territory. One response of a nesting pair to an intruding eagle is to circle above the trespasser until it departs. Most commonly, though, the pair will chase the interloper. Such territorial chases continue until the vagrant leaves. If the defending eagle feels the situation warrants it,

it may even attack with talons extended, striking the invader on the back or wing. The most spectacular defense is known as whirling. As the attacking eagle swoops down upon the intruder, the lower bird rolls over in flight presenting its talons. The two birds grasp talons and cartwheel earthward, releasing their grip as they near the surface. Interestingly, whirling is also thought to be part of the courtship display—proving that the old adage "war between the sexes" may be an accurate description!

Such physical contacts are rare, and bald eagles reserve them mostly for other adult bald eagles, since the threat of competition is greatest from those of your own kind. Breeding bald eagles show more tolerance toward immature eagles that wander into their territory, perhaps because non-breeding juveniles don't present as much competition for space and food as would other breeding adults.

OTHER INTERLOPERS

While other birds, especially large raptors, are sometimes at odds with bald eagles, they do not usually elicit a strong defensive response. An exception would be the fish-eating osprey, from which the bald eagle often steals, and whose presence bald eagles won't tolerate. Some researchers feel that bald eagles so vigorously exclude ospreys from their territories that they reduce the fish hawk's nesting success.

Ospreys are more tolerant of humans than are bald eagles, and will nest on lakes where human activity levels exceed the eagle's tolerance. In these cases, osprey numbers sometime

exceed those that are found in similar, but pristine, habitats that also include the shy bald eagle, lending credence to the theory that bald eagles do indeed drive ospreys out, or, at the very least, that ospreys can flourish in the absence of bald eagles.

There is one intruder that the bald eagle does not drive away: humans. Those pairs that nest in a true wilderness setting are particularly sensitive to human intrusion. Nests are sometimes abandoned when human activity exceeds the eagle's tolerance. In some locations, habitat that might otherwise support eagle pairs is empty of them simply because of people pressure. Research indicates that easily accessible lakes with a high amount of recreational use, especially power boating, nearly always have lower nesting densities than similar pristine lakes. Those pairs with low tolerance for humans simply move out. Heavy human use on a lake can even affect those eagles that decide to stay, since the presence of people can disrupt feeding, which increases stress and may lower productivity. When humans compete with the eagles for food sources through recreational or commercial fishing, the birds may suffer from the loss of, or change in, their prey base.

There is some evidence that eagles can grow to tolerate a certain level of human presence. Some pairs switch to nest sites farther inland from the busy waterway to find the solitude they need. And in a few cases, bald eagles have been known to continue nesting in their traditional territory even after low level human uses, such as cabins, have been constructed very near their nest site. These exceptions

should not be used to justify encroachment in eagle habitat. If the activity continues for more than one season, the pair may permanently leave the area.

Though we may find it difficult to measure or define the size and shape of an eagle pair's territory, the birds themselves have evolved a means of defining and protecting it through both aggressive and ritual display. Their motives are simple and ones we can easily understand; to secure for their nesting effort a monopoly of food resources, and to insure the safety of their offspring. That eagles will tolerate each other on the wintering grounds, at food sources where prey is plentiful (such as a salmon spawning run), and within the larger home range indicates that they are not anti-social, but motivated by a strong evolutionary urge to control those factors near their nest that affect their reproduction.

The one factor they can't control is how humans change the places they call home. Only through continued efforts by concerned people to protect those resources the eagle requires, through the limitation of development or providing the eagles with buffer zones around their territory, will this bird continue to survive. Though in many ways the bald eagle is an amazingly adaptable animal, it cannot escape the evolutionary imprint of its nesting needs. Even if all other factors, such as suitable nest sites and an availability of food, are present, an eagle population can't long exist in a region devoid of solitude.

CHAPTER FOUR

ROOM AND BOARD

*S*plit around a granite island outcrop, the twin cataracts of Lower Basswood Falls poured noisily into Crooked Lake. Flecks of foam swirled on the dark waters, catching for a few minutes in the strong current at the base of the falls before being carried away by the chop into the lake.

From my perch on the high rocks near our ranger base, I could scan up the narrow entrance of Crooked Lake and see where the gradually exhausted current caressed a small island of towering pines before deflecting north along the narrow channel toward Wednesday Bay.

A small sucker bobbed belly up on the water's surface. The white underside of the bottom-feeding fish gleamed against the dark lake among the swirling back eddies. Caught in the powerful current above the falls and carried into the tumult, the fish had been dashed to its death and now bounced lazily along the island's face, spinning and drifting ever farther north.

Above this narrow section of Crooked Lake, where tall billowy pines and pinnacled spruce scraped green against the blue summer sky, an adult bald eagle soared. I watched its easy circles, the effortless minutes of gliding between single wing beats, and saw as it deftly canted its glaring white tail left or right in a silent

maneuver to change direction. Ever tighter the circles grew until I was sure that the bird had seen the floundering fish.

Drifting down the eagle alighted in the dead, twisted branches of a lightning killed Norway pine. The fish floated 50 yards away. The eagle sat nonchalantly, as if ignoring the morsel, and I wondered if perhaps the hunting had been too good lately for the bird to be bothered with scooping up a sucker.

I needn't have worried. With a powerful downstroke of its wings, the eagle leaped from its perch, launched out over the lake, and took a few strokes toward the fish. Lower it glided, and as it swooped nearly to the lake's surface, the dark wings folded slightly back as yellow legs and feet reached forward to snag the fish. I was impressed.

Turning from me the eagle flew over the misty waterfalls to a stand of lofty pines upstream. It circled once over the tallest trees with the fish in its talons, and then dropped from sight to its well hidden nest where its mate and offspring waited.

∽

FINDING FOOD

Room and board doesn't always come so easily for bald eagles, although the wisest birds seem to have a knack for locating their territory where food will be found easily. Like the eagles in Wednesday Bay a few miles to the north, the pair near our ranger camp had located near moving water. And like those eagles farther up the lake, this pair had also been observed feeding on yet another waterlogged, winter-killed moose. Their nest near the falls served as a base from which they could feed near the swirling waters. On many occasions we had watched them fish from perches below the falls.

There is likely some significance to the fact that they hunted more frequently below the falls. Just as the sucker had been swept to its doom, many other creatures shared a similar fate. No doubt the success of this pair of eagles depended, to a certain extent, on the frequency of such events.

Bald eagles are wonderfully well adapted to their environment, displaying a versatility uncommon in most birds of prey. For instance, some research suggests that northerly nesting pairs that choose territories where moving water can be found upon their return in the spring, produce more offspring than do eagles in the same region nesting near still (and therefore possibly still frozen) waters. The speculation is that when they first arrive from the south to find the lakes locked in ice, these open, moving waters provide access to food. Our observation of

carrion moose, and fish swept over the falls, seems to confirm this. Although the relationship of abundant food early in the season to nesting success has not been difinitively proved, the connection appears strong.

The relationship between food and the breeding success of other large, northern nesting birds, such as snow and Canada geese, is documented. Geese that have fed on high quality forage arrive at the nesting grounds in better condition, lay larger clutches of eggs, and have a higher ratio of viable eggs. Eagles, too, feed on their way north, but should they arrive in less than ideal condition, the immediate availability of food could conceivably enhance their nesting activities. In addition to carrion that may be present near moving water, many fish species make spring spawning runs in these streams, during which they are vulnerable to the eagles.

This proclivity may be yet another example of the long evolutionary process that has favored those eagles that are adept at choosing territories near important food sources, and eagles that will feed on a variety of prey. This flexibility has allowed bald eagles to expertly exploit their environment for their energy needs. And that need is fairly great.

ENERGY NEEDS AND CONSERVATION

Because bald eagles are such large birds, they need a great deal of food. An average adult bald eagle requires between 450 and 550 calories per day; that is about 20 percent of your caloric needs. The larger the individual eagle, the more food they require. Northern bald eagles, which are larger than their southern counterparts, require more food. However, because of Bergmann's Rule, these larger birds are also more energy efficient, and so as their body size increases, their energy needs increase more slowly. In other words, though a northern eagle's weight may be twice that of a southern cousin, its energy needs would be less than double. The larger eagle is more efficient at conserving energy because it has proportionally less surface area to body mass.

How much and how often they eat can be influenced by weather. When conditions are cold and windy, eagles need to consume more food to supply their energy needs. The highest energy needs occur when wind combines with rain or snow, penetrating the bird's feathers causing rapid heat loss.

To reduce their food needs during very cold weather, bald eagles spend more time roosting, since the act of flying burns considerable energy. Winter conditions may dictate that they fly only about one percent of the day, choosing to conserve energy by perching during the remainder.

Besides increasing their roosting time, bald eagles have other strategies to reduce food needs. Soaring is a prime example. By riding upwelling air currents, eagles need to exert themselves only minimally. Bald eagles can also adjust their metabolic rate, a process known as thermoregulation. This metabolic adjustment takes place both at night and in response to weather conditions, allowing the bird to conserve up to five percent of its daily energy needs.

Another adaptation is the ability to gorge, a practice found in many

other predators. Because a predator can't always control the conditions surrounding the hunt or the movements of prey, most can feed heavily when food is present and survive for several days when rations are lean. In the presence of abundant food, bald eagles gorge themselves, storing the excess in a pocket in their esophagus known as a crop. A full crop is obvious by the marked bulge in the bird's throat, and it stores nourishment for several days.

FORAGING STRATEGIES

Still, they must inevitably feed, and the bald eagle does so by scavenging, stealing, and hunting. Their preferred food throughout their range is fish, but they also kill small mammals and waterfowl. Because they so willingly scavenge, which they seem to prefer to hunting, bald eagles can take advantage of food sources unavailable to them through hunting. Not many other birds of prey share this adaptation, an evolved trait that has insured that the bald eagle is among the most proficient at extracting food value from its environment. Deer, moose, elk, bison, whales, and other marine mammals all provide carrion meals—size has no bearing when the prey is already dead. In this category falls domestic livestock. Sheep and cattle that have died due to weather or disease occasionally make a meal for a scavenging eagle. No doubt this has led to the misconception that eagles kill livestock.

In addition, they are adept at stealing food from each other and other birds of prey, particularly the osprey. Both stealing and scavenging require a lower expenditure of energy than does hunting.

Not only does this diversity help insure an individual bald eagle's survival, it also allows for the species to be successful across large portions of the continent. Because many species of birds or animals are extremely selective in their food source, they can exist only in its vicinity. Dramatic declines in these creature's populations can occur when their singular food source becomes unavailable due to bad weather or other uncontrollable factors. The bald eagle's foraging flexibility helps to insure its success.

Stealing food is a highly evolved art with the bald eagle. When a bald eagle steals from its own kind, scientists call it pirating; when they steal from other species, it is labeled kleptoparasitism. Regardless of what one calls it, this is not a moral defect, as Benjamin Franklin thought, but is a trait with evolutionary roots. The advantage seems obvious; stealing can be easier than hunting, although there are instances when the effort expended by an eagle to wrest food from a competitor seemingly outweighs the benefits. Even when abundant food is present, such as in the Pacific Northwest where spent salmon carcasses litter the stream during spawning runs, bald eagles will rush other eagles that are feeding on a carcass. Apparently the stealing urge is so strong that they may ignore plentiful food, and is probably based on some deep seated inherited competitive trait. Over the eons of natural selection, eagles proficient at stealing probably were most successful in surviving, and passed this trait on to their offspring. Developed to an undeniable urge, bald eagles seem

to practice stealing even when unnecessary.

Larger eagles tend to steal more often than small ones. This may be true simply because largeness is an aid in intimidating a rival, or it may be because a big eagle needs more food and is therefore more likely to be hungry. Hunger is great motivation.

Stealing can result in some of the bald eagle's most visually dramatic behavior. When attempting to steal food from another eagle, the attacker may give chase through the air, harassing the other bird in an aerial dogfight until it drops the meal. Occasionally an eagle will plummet from the heavens to dive upon victims that are already on the ground, although they usually intentionally miss, pulling up in a noisy flurry of feathers. If successful in its harrying, the attacker will usurp the morsel when the victim flees. When both eagles are on the ground, the attacker may walk or trot in an ungainly bounce toward the feeding eagle in hops of intimidation. The thief may escalate the raucous squabble by jumping upon the victim, grasping talons with it, or tugging at the food. Occasionally they use their beaks as weapons. The beleaguered defender may try to cover the food with wings outstretched, a maneuver known as mantling.

Just because a bald eagle may be prone to stealing, doesn't mean it will always choose that route. Sometimes they will share a kill willingly with each other, or even other species. On occasion, especially on the wintering grounds, bald eagles will take turns catching fish concentrated below dams.

While a bald eagle will eat just about anything, when given a choice of foods, it will usually select fish. Just about any species of fish may end as a meal for eagles, but there seems a tendency toward those species that frequent shallow water or are surface feeders, and are therefore vulnerable to the eagle. Species of fish that typically inhabit deep water probably only end up in the eagle's diet when they die or float injured to the surface where they can be scavenged. By studying fish remains scattered around the base of the nest tree, researchers can gain good insight into the eagle's diet. Surprisingly, some pairs nesting on the same lake may show decidedly different fish preferences, which could either indicate the relative abundance of various fish species within the pairs' feeding territory, or an individual's mastery of a skill needed to capture that specific species.

Rules, they say, are made to be broken, and just because most breeding bald eagles subsist primarily on fish, doesn't mean that there aren't some well-documented exceptions. Eagles that nest near colonies of shore birds feed extensively on them. In Maryland's Blackwater Marshes, nesting eagles prey heavily on waterfowl and muskrats. Even those eagles that feed primarily on fish will switch to other prey as they become seasonally available. Bald eagles frequently feed on migrating waterfowl that congregate during the flight south. Waterfowl injured from the rigors of migration or crippled by hunters, fall prey to eagles. Ducks, geese and swans are also particularly susceptible to disease when in crowded conditions, such as on waterfowl refuges, and like most predators, bald eagles are very adept at recognizing the abnormal behavior of sick or

injured prey. Even waterfowl as large as Canada geese become meals for the bald eagle.

Though bald eagles will attack and kill small mammals, it is their least preferred regular food source. As always, there are exceptions, and those eagles that winter in parts of Utah feed extensively on jackrabbits, hunting them in much the same manner as does the golden eagle.

HUNTING SKILLS

The bald eagle's head may not be bald, but its legs are, with feathers ending two inches from the toes. Bare feet and lower legs may be an adaptation to avoid wet feathers, which seems reasonable for an eagle that spends so much time near water. The legs of the bald eagle are long and powerful, terminating in feet equipped with four toes. The three front toes grasp backward where they meet the single forward reaching toe. All the toes are tipped with a talon of about two inches. On the underside of the toes are spicules; rough knobs that help the bird grasp slippery prey.

Though the eagle's incredible sight gives it the ability to spot prey, when it comes to capturing or killing, the real weapons are the talons, which can wreak terrible damage on their prey. Aside from the stunning impact of just being hit by such a fast, large bird, the feet can exert a tremendously powerful grip. Once the eagle grasps its prey, the muscles of the leg contort, causing tendons to contract and talons to tighten, driving them deep into the vitals of the victim. The pressure is very literally bone-crushing. The contractions that close the talons also lock

them in place, making it unlikely that prey will wiggle loose. This same feature allows the bald eagle to securely clench a roosting branch, even while it sleeps.

Bald eagles hunt both alone and in cooperation. A common hunting technique is to watch for fish while soaring. Shorelines and coastlines create the wind currents that are critical to the eagle's soaring success. While gliding along, whether from a height or near the surface, eagles are constantly watching for dead or dying fish. Similarly, they frequently use their perching trees as vantage points from which they can spot prey. Eagles often choose their perch site with a view of a windward shore to take advantage of the wave action in washing up prey. When a morsel is observed, the eagle generally glides to it quickly, dropping at the last minute to grasp it in its talons. Like other raptors, the bald eagle can plummet quickly by tucking in its wings in a maneuver known as a stoop. Whiffling is another technique used to rapidly lose altitude, during which the bird tilts sideways to slip air from beneath its wings.

Unlike the osprey that may immerse itself completely when attacking a fish, eagles generally prefer to reach out with one or both legs and grab the fish while it is at the surface. Since a bald eagle can't lift anything much over four pounds, and would struggle with something half their body weight, they are occasionally forced to swim ashore if the fish is too large. Using its powerful wings as oars, the eagle rows to land.

When fish are trapped in small pools or are in shallow water while spawning, bald eagles pursue them

much in the manner of a wading bird, sometimes wading up to their breasts in water. Once the prey is spotted and cornered, the eagle dips its head beneath the water and grabs the fish with its beak.

Bald eagles will also hunt on the ground, though it is an uncommon method. Some eagles stroll through Alaskan seabird colonies, consuming the chicks. There are even reports of bald eagles excavating seabird burrows. Ever the opportunist, bald eagles seem to recognize the food value presented by a rising flood, and stalk along the water's edge, grabbing rodents and mammals that swim to shore. Along northern reaches of the partially frozen Mississippi River, bald eagles walk along the edge of the ice, grabbing gizzard shad from the open water. They have even been known to inch up on a birthing sea lion to grab the placenta after the pup has been born.

While hunting rabbits in the sagebrush of south Utah, bald eagles stroll through the cover in an attempt to flush the game. When the rabbit runs, the eagle will launch itself into the air and pursue on wing, striking the rabbit and pinning it to the earth. Rabbits also present an instance when bald eagles will hunt cooperatively. While one bird stalks, another strikes the blow when the prey tries to escape.

Similar techniques have been noted when bald eagles hunt waterfowl. Working together, they harry a flock of ducks, coots, or geese. As one eagle saves energy by soaring or perching, another dives on the flock. They switch off until they have tired the prey, and then one will move in for a kill. It has been observed that eagles will sometime work together to pursue a flying flock of ducks or geese, repeatedly worrying the flock until a victim becomes separated and killed. In this case, the eagle will come in for the kill from below, rolling on its back to attack with its talons. Such skill when hunting swift flying waterfowl attests to both the maneuverability and speed that an attacking eagle can generate.

Other interesting reports reveal that the eagle ingeniously uses terrain to hide its approach, such as flying behind embankments or in the troughs of waves at sea, rising suddenly over to attack. Incredibly, there are reports of eagles stealing food from sea otters. As the floating, relaxed otter uses its furry chest as dinner table, an eagle flies in quietly from behind only inches above the ocean. The eagle suddenly snatches the morsel from what surely must be a very startled otter.

I've observed eagles methodically drift over rafts of diving ducks until the waterfowl are in a tight knot. Often the ducks dive in response to the eagle's presence, but invariably they must surface for air. The constant harassment by the eagle begins to tire the ducks, and the length of time they can stay under water begins to decrease. As the birds tire, the eagle will swoop down to grab one of the least wary. Injured ducks invariably keep to the shorelines of marshes where they can find shelter in the emergent vegetation. Here the eagle will course low and slowly, trying to flush the crippled bird toward a watery opening where it can be attacked. One quiet Wisconsin lake on which I duck hunt has a resident pair of bald eagles. While I've sat for hours in a duck blind

for my chance at a duck, I've noticed the pair intently watching rafted ducks from their perch trees, or coursing the shorelines in the manner described. They are incredibly patient and apparently exert very little effort for their daily duck dinner.

Like most predators, eagles are astute observers of their preys' behavior, watching carefully until they descry the abnormal behavior of the sick or injured. They may also use the behavior of non-prey neighboring creatures to give clues as to the whereabouts of food. The cries of ravens or crows at carrion can draw the eagle's attention. Eagles diligently watch other fish-eating birds, such as gulls and mergansers, for indications of gathering fish, or in the hopes of stealing their catch. One of the more astounding relationships between bald eagles and another species was reported along the coast of British Columbia. Here, the eagles joined another skilled predator, the killer whale, in pursuing schools of salmon. Fish forced to the surface by the whales were caught by eagles.

SUCCESS RATE

Until they perfect hunting skills, young bald eagles depend heavily on carrion. Because of their shape, immature bald eagles are especially efficient soarers, and they use this to their advantage by wandering on the wind in search of food. Conversely, adult bald eagles, though also skilled at soaring, are at a disadvantage in weak thermals. They spend more time actively hunting, much of which is done from a perch.

The nature of the quarry, the conditions surrounding the hunt, the

age of the hunter, and perhaps even the sex has much to do with the eagle's hunting success rate. And it would be fair to assume that eagles, like people, come with varying levels of skills. Studies done show an extremely wide range of success, from a low of 28 percent to a high of 72. But don't forget that hunting is only part of the bald eagle's foraging strategy. By virtue of their diet diversity, and through the common practices of stealing and scavenging, bald eagles take advantage of a variety of foods.

Suffice it to say that eagles have evolved ample skills and strategies to find food. Whether it be the selection of a nest site near good fishing waters, or the aerial agility needed to attack fleeing prey, eons of natural selection have left this grand bird with the eyesight and acumen needed to be widely successful.

That bald eagles are found across such a wide range in North America says much about their adaptability to varying conditions. Though our vision of them is often that of a skilled hunter streaking from the heavens to snatch a fish from the water, even their scavenging skills are to be admired. In a fine illustration of nature's intricate web of life, the bald eagle turns what we would consider foul waste, the carrion of the world, into a creature of majesty and power.

CHAPTER FIVE

A ROOM WITH A VIEW

. . . .

*F*ar aloft the bald eagle swung slowly, inscribing great circles in the pale June sky. Through field glasses we watched as its broad wings tipped through the arc, while its bright white tail twisted slightly as a rudder. Against the blue, each wing's dark primary feathers were clearly defined, like fingers on a hand flexed wide.

Resting after a 10-mile paddle, we floated on the bay's tranquil waters as the first really warm day of summer blew gently against our winter-white skin. Herring gulls screamed and laughed near their rookery island. Binoculars held to our eyes, we lay back in the canoe watching the gulls and watching the eagle. Like lizards on a rock we luxuriated in the warmth, and as we did, the eagle soared above the lakeland wilderness, riding the rising thermals. A light chop slopped cheerily against the side of the drifting canoe.

The eagle began to descend in tightening circles, easing down toward the east shore of the bay where hills of jumbled spruce, pine, aspen, and birch rose from the reed-clad shore. Near the crest of that ridge a monarch white pine stood, its billowing crown climbing above the surrounding forest, and beneath its shelter hunkered a dark mass, the largest of the pair's three nests. Toward this tree the graceful bird tipped and twisted, drifting like an autumn leaf in a breeze.

AN EYE TOWARD
EASE AND COMFORT

Most bald eagle nests share common characteristics, and it seems as though the species of tree is less important than its shape and attributes. Whatever the species, the tree must be large and alive, although trees with damaged tops are common. Whereas ospreys may prefer dead trees, bald eagles rarely choose one. However, if their traditional nest tree dies, they may continue to use it unless it can no longer support the nest.

Usually the selected nest tree will be the tallest in its vicinity. The pair will choose to build their nest in the crotch of stout branches about a third of the way down from the treetop, but still above the surrounding forest canopy. Truly old trees may afford the eagles a nest location as high as 200 feet above the ground, and even typical nests will be at a height of somewhere between 25 and 70 feet.

This lofty location is no accident. Such height offers the pair a vantage point from which to survey their territory, and with their bright white heads and the nest's prominent location, declare their occupancy. Nest trees usually have some deformity to the crown. Together, the site's height and the crown's deformity allow for passage in and out of the nest. Not that every big nest you see in a tall, shoreline tree will belong to bald eagles. Chances are if the nest you spot is near the crown of the tree, it belongs to an osprey pair.

Besides proclaiming territorial ownership and providing a vantage point from which the eagle pair can watch for food or intruders, the nest's height may furnish them with a breeze to help alleviate insects that could torment the young. It is also very possible that nests favored with a breeze make it easier for fledglings to learn to fly as they hop and hover in the anxious weeks before their first true flight.

But a view and a breeze aren't enough to make a tree a candidate for an eagle nest. Bald eagle pairs wisely choose a tree with a large crown that adds an umbrella effect. Besides shielding the nest and its occupants from rain, a full crown insures shade, an important consideration for hatchlings unable to regulate their body temperature. And although northern eagles will have long since migrated, the crown may also serve to deflect heavy winter snow that could collapse the nest.

BIG BIRDS, BIG NESTS,
BIG TREES

Matching the grandness of their size, bald eagles build some of the largest nests of any species, and certainly the biggest in North America. The largest bird nest of any kind ever recorded was built by bald eagles at St. Petersburg, Florida. A staggering 9 1/2 feet across by 20 feet deep, this monument to years of nest building is estimated to have weighed more than two tons. Even an average nest, which is generally about five feet across by three feet deep, can weigh hundreds of pounds. Given these dimensions and weight, eagles are careful to choose a tree capable of supporting it all.

While bald eagles sometimes make do with lesser trees, large old trees are usually preferred. Imagine the stress placed upon a chosen nesting tree. It must withstand hundreds of

pounds of nest, swaying far above the earth in a tossing wind. It would be more than just an inconvenience for a pair to lose their nest to a collapse. Such an accident could cause the loss of an entire clutch or brood. Evolution then has programmed bald eagles to build in the biggest and stoutest trees they can find.

As in its foraging strategy, the bald eagle displays a flexibility in tree species selection. In our ranger territory, and across the Great Lakes region, favored trees are generally large white or red pines. Pines are also a common nest tree in the northeast. Florida eagles choose either a pine or a big cypress. Ponderosa and lodgepole pines serve the eagles of the inland west, while Douglas firs and Sitka spruce are particularly favored in the Pacific Northwest. Large hardwoods may be chosen in some regions, such as cottonwood on Kodiak Island or aspen in Saskatchewan. In the complete absence of trees, such as on the tundra, bald eagles will build mound nests on the ground. They also occasionally nest on cliffs, much in the manner of the golden eagle. A Baja California pair even nested on a giant cactus! Ouch.

Unfortunately, the eagle's preferred forest sentinel trees are now rare and growing rarer. In the upper Midwest and the East, monarch trees that survived the logging era are not numerous and are indispensable to eagle nesting. While most of these remnant giants are now enjoying some kind of protection (when on public land), especially if they are located in an eagle pair's territory or contain a nest, even these behemoths will someday topple. They are not easily

replaced, and preparing for that day takes vision. Forest managers and wildlife biologists must plan far into the future to insure that some of today's young trees grow to advanced age if there is any hope of preserving quality habitat for the bald eagle.

Eagles have been known to nest on artificial structures; both those designed for this purpose and those merely handy. However, it is a rare occurrence, and, in this regard, the bald eagle does not seem very adaptable. Unlike the osprey, which readily takes to artificial nest sites situated on tall poles (which resemble the bare, dead trees they prefer), the bald eagle perhaps can't overcome the eons of evolution that have programmed it to choose trees with certain attributes that we are only now beginning to understand. Even once we understand them, it is unlikely that any among us can build something even approximating a towering white pine, or even a common aspen.

MORE THAN A MASS OF STICKS

Because bald eagles are territorial, long-lived, and mostly monogamous, they use particularly good nest sites for years, even decades. Some sites may even be used by a succession of pairs. There are credible reports of the same nest being used for nearly 70 years, although the average nest survives for a much shorter time. In Saskatchewan, where the relatively weak and short-lived trembling aspen is a frequent nest tree, many nests are destroyed after five years. Where larger, stronger trees are available, the average nest lifespan may be nearer 20

years. With each passing year the occupants repair and add onto the nest, until it grows to astounding proportions. Eventually the nest collapses from its own weight, or the support branches give way. Occasionally the entire tree blows over.

Because nests are generally long-lived, nest building is infrequent. One may easily watch a robin build its annual nest, but because of the sporadic nature of eagle nest construction, many field biologists have waited long years to view an eagle pair taking on this task. Based on reports of these patient observers around the continent, it seems as though somewhere in its range, eagles are building a nest during just about any month of the year. Though most mated pairs will construct their nest (or repair an old one) in the spring, just before laying their eggs, some nests are built in the fall and winter as well. Perhaps some pairs just believe in planning ahead.

Summer nest building is usually done by unmated pairs, or pairs who have lost their clutch or nest. Researchers believe that nest building by those nonbreeding eagles may be a means of strengthening or maintaining the pair pond. Though I've not read any speculation about it, it seems that nest building in the summer could be a means of establishing territory. There is no better time to discern which areas are occupied by rivals than during the nesting season.

The pair begins refurbishing an established nest or building a new one as as soon as they arrive from their wintering grounds. It is a task shared by both sexes. The pair can complete repairs, or even build a new nest, in as little as four days. They pick up sticks and grass from the ground and fly the materials to the nest site. Bald eagles even snap branches from trees by leaping skyward with a branch clasped in their powerful feet. Whatever the source of the stick, the eagle places each one precisely, weaving the nest much like a wicker basket. Females perform most of this work. Once sufficient sticks are entwined, the pair switches to retrieving softer and finer materials. Sedges, grass, pine needles and moss are used to create a deep, soft mat in which a 10- to 14-inch cup is formed. It is in this cup that the female will lay her eggs.

Nest shape varies depending upon the formation of the tree in which it is built. In coniferous trees with a web of stout, flat limbs lying parallel to the ground, the eagle nest may be relatively flat and disk shaped. If the trunk diverges widely into several upright members, eagles will build a bowl or cone-shaped nest cradled between these supports. If the tree offers just a simple Y-shaped fork where the arms are upright and parallel, the pair will build a long, cylindrical nest. No matter the shape, the nest must be large and sturdy enough to support the weight of the entire family through a short but busy summer. Throughout that summer, the adults will continue to haul fresh nest material, increasing the nest depth and weight.

ALTERNATE NESTS AND OTHER MYSTERIES

As did the eagles of Wednesday Bay, many pairs also construct one or two alternate nests. Most of these alternate nests will be less than a

mile from the primary site, and are often only a few hundred yards distant. Those scientists that concern themselves with such things have speculated about the occurrence of these alternate nests, though it is likely only the eagles know the real reason they build them. Some researchers theorize that because eagles first must satisfy a nest-building urge before laying eggs, alternate sites are sometimes constructed to meet that need. Still others have wondered if the alternate nests are not a means of reducing nest parasites. By switching nests occasionally, the parasites hosted by an active nest's build-up of organic trash (feces, bits of food, etc.) would be starved out.

Perhaps the most logical reason is that these alternate nests are a safeguard used by pairs who arrive in the spring nearly ready to lay eggs and find their primary site unusable or destroyed. These alternate nests may also provide a location to lay a second clutch, which many eagles will do, if the first nest and eggs are destroyed early in the nesting season. And it is possible that these conspicuous extra nests serve as yet another means by which the very territorial bald eagle warns others of its ownership of that particular piece of property.

Included in this range of difficult-to-interpret eagle behavior is the bird's strange habit of decorating its nest. In Minnesota's Chippewa National Forest, eagle researchers have noted that almost every nest contained a sprig of fresh, green, white pine, even though red pines outnumbered the white. Elsewhere, eagles routinely place some type of greenery atop their nest, as if in decoration. Depending on the type of greenery, there may be some medicinal or insect repelling qualities. Researchers have speculated that this periodic delivery of greenery, like buying flowers for your spouse, may be another means of bolstering the pair bond.

But the strange deliveries don't end there. Many nests contain some unusual white or bright object. Bleach bottles, golf balls, light bulbs—all manner of bizarre things—have found their way into an eagle's nest. Eagles may have mistaken these white objects for the pale belly of an overturned, floating fish. What isn't explainable is that not only do the eagles haul these unusual items to their home, where they must determine they are inedible, but they keep them in the nest and have even been observed tossing them about in play.

The miracle of eagle architecture lies in their ability to build massive structures. It also lies in their instinct to search for and choose a tree of particular attributes at a site that will serve the needs of the mated pair and the offspring to come. Evolution would have it no other way. The millennia have selected those birds with the skills needed to build and repair such nests, and has implanted in their mind a picture of the perfect tree to guide their search. As long as there are bald eagles and wild places with towering trees and fish-filled waters, and as long as we give the birds the peace they need, this picture will not fail them in their quest. And it must not, for the building of nests is not about architectural beauty. It is about the most important drive the eagle ever experiences: reproduction.

CHAPTER SIX

FROM EGG TO EAGLE

. . . .

I t was raining fish, so to speak. Swooping precisely into the gap between the pine's crown and the nest, the adult eagle then turned swiftly in a flurry of wings and shot back out from the tree. On the descent into the gap the great bird carried the headless remains of a four-pound northern pike. On its way out, its talons were empty.

On the edge of the nest sat its mate, who pounced on the sudden delivery. Shoulders and head barely visible to us above the nest's enormous wall of sticks, we watched as this bird tore bits of flesh from the carcass. With each tidbit the bird tipped out of view into the depths of the nest.

Though we couldn't see what was occurring within the nest, we could guess. We could imagine the gray, downy chicks with dark beaks open and heads back, screeching demands for food. Dwarfed by their parent, but giants of insistence, the nestlings whined. Gentle beyond its size, the adult bird presented morsels to the insatiable chicks, consuming the fish within minutes.

On that moist day when the air lay damp on our skin and the water heaved thickly like syrup, we could only speculate about the feeding ritual. But we did not have to guess about the source of the food. Behind an ancient granite shelf spearing far out into Wednesday Bay, a dark promontory known locally as Pancake

Point, we had slipped noiselessly along in our canoe. Not a whisper of air stirred. Only the rhythm of our canoe paddles and the hushed flump of our small bow wave betrayed our presence.

As we turned past the rocky tip toward the wider expanse of Wednesday Bay, we were startled to see a mature bald eagle standing on the dark shelf of rock at the water's edge. Beneath its yellow feet lay a fish, pale belly turned toward us. A shocked white head shot up from feeding to face us.

Eagle and people froze. The canoe coasted nearer. Tense with indecision, the eagle watched us, its yellow eyes glaring, rigid as the rock on which it stood, its piercing gaze riveted on mine. The stare of an eagle is penetrating. The black talons of one yellow foot clenched the partially consumed northern pike. The stare-down continued for long seconds, and after the shock of the encounter left us, I began to worry about frightening the eagle from its meal. Without a word between us, both thinking the same thought, Mary Jo and I dipped our paddles quietly, easing the canoe away.

Once our backs were to the bird we heard the extraordinarily loud compression of air beneath broad wings, palpable on this thick day. We turned toward the sound. The eagle had leaped into the air, each wing stroke audible as it whooshed low along the jumbled shore. Not forgotten, the pike dangled from the eagle's talons.

Perhaps a city block from us down the shore, the eagle reared back and swept suddenly upward into a gnarled snag, where it landed and froze. I dug my bandana from my back pocket, wiped the steamy air from my eyeglasses, fumbled in our pack for a pair of binoculars, and finally turned them toward the eagle. It had resumed its lunch. Its yellow scimitar beak ripped at the head of the carcass. I put the binoculars on the flat of a paddle and passed them to Mary Jo. After just a few more minutes of feeding, the eagle pitched from its perch with wings wide and glided east toward the nest.

Rowing slowly in the viscous air the eagle sluggishly gained altitude until it was above the ridge and the pinnacle pine that contained the pair's nest. Counting ourselves very fortunate, we watched as the dutiful parent delivered the pike to its family.

But not until after, we noted, it had had a bite of lunch for itself.

PAIR BONDS

As any parent can attest, it takes concerted effort to successfully raise young ones. Bald eagles are no slackers in that department, for the pair bond runs deep and the instinct to reproduce is strong. The breeding season is a busy one, and it takes the efforts of both eagle parents if the young are going to survive.

Bald eagle pairs are devoted to each other and their offspring. While many believe that the eagle's pair bond is life-long, this is only an assumption. It has never been proven that bald eagles mate for life, though it is known that their relationships are long-lived and generally monogamous. If it seems like this is splitting hairs, the difference is important. A life-long bond does not allow for a change in partners should one mate prove unsatisfactory. It has been suggested by some eagle researchers that these birds do sometimes "divorce" each other if they fail to produce viable eggs, or if they fail at another point in the reproductive cycle.

Evolution is not anthropomorphic. Though we may wish eagles to be always steadfast and faithful (which they seem to be when the pair is compatible), survival dictates that wasted reproductive efforts require a change. Risking repeat failure is evolutionary folly. A life-long bond, or at the least one of lengthy duration, is one survival strategy that allows for successful mates to continue that success, and would be selected by evolution. It seems equally likely that nature would also provide for an option of divorce should unsatisfactory couplings take place so that genetic potential would not needlessly be wasted.

That aside, most pairs do seem to remain together for many years. Bald eagles mature sexually and receive their adult plumage at the age of four, which is not likely a coincidence. Many birds use dramatic plumage to attract mates, and the distinctive coloration of the adult bald eagle may serve the same function, or at least advertise sexual maturity. Though many bald eagles will mate at the age of four years, there is evidence to indicate that in parts of their range some bald eagles choose not to reproduce until the age of six. Not much is known about how bald eagles select each other, or even during what time of the year this selection occurs. Since some birds remain unmated for a year or two after first sporting their adult coloration, it may be that there are many subtleties in this process of which we are unaware, and that accounts for the long delay in mating.

During the winter season, when many bald eagles are far from their nesting territories, they often gather en masse to fish or scavenge. At that time they will roost together in select locations. Wintering ground congregations bring eagles from diverse ranges together, and it is conceivable that during such gatherings unmated birds search for a prospective mate. Selecting a new mate from those gathered at the wintering grounds also could bring together eagles of widely separated gene pools, which is generally considered an advantage, whereas selection from those in one's own home territory may raise the possibility of breeding with relatives. Interestingly, mated pairs do not depart wintering area together, and they may arrive at the nest site at different times. It is a

strange bond that allows pairs to avoid migrating together, yet binds them to a common destination.

COURTSHIP AND COUPLING

Once the pair does arrive in its territory, both eagles face the busy task of building or remodeling their nest. That doesn't mean that romance is dead. Though they may have long ago selected each other, each mating season sees a new round of courtship that is a necessary prelude to copulation.

Though few have seen them, the courtship rituals of bald eagles are both spectacular and athletic, adding a new dimension to the phrase "romance is in the air." Whirling displays, during which the pair grasps talons and cartwheels in union toward the earth, is the most majestic. Only as a crash to earth looms imminently do they release their embrace. Other romantic antics include a corkscrew chase display, during which one eagle flies beneath the other while rolled on its back, reaching up with its feet to touch its mate. Sometimes the two exchange places and repeat the display.

Observations of captive bald eagles reveal that courting pairs perch together for a time, after which one or the other may initiate sex. Delicately using their massive beaks, the pair takes turns stroking each other around the neck, back, shoulder and breast. Often the female will crouch and call in a distinctive, low voice to her mate. With her wings somewhat open and her body horizontal, she indicates to her mate that she is receptive. The male may respond by moving his tail up and down, flapping his wings, and calling loudly. Sometimes these overtures and seemingly loving caresses lead to copulation, but not always.

When the eagles do decide to join, the male carefully hops upon the female's back, balling up his sharp talons to protect his mate. With the male thus awkwardly perched, wings flapping occasionally for balance, the female rotates her tail to near vertical, giving her mate access to her cloaca. Thus exposed, the male responds by lowering his tail until he can press his cloaca to hers and transfer his semen. Both sexes use this same vent for excretion.

The fresh morning hours seem to be the preferred time for these brief unions, which may last only 10 seconds and rarely exceed a minute or two. After copulation the pair may continue their tender ways by perching together to preen, or they may fly off together to prepare the nest for the virtually inevitable results of their copulation. Though occasionally pairs may copulate during the fall, most unions take place six days prior to the laying of the first egg and may recur during the laying process, ceasing when the laying of eggs ends. Once the busy incubating and rearing season commences, sex between mated pairs is a thing of the past.

EGG LAYING AND INCUBATION

In the deep, soft bowl of her massive nest, the female bald eagle will lay one to three dull white eggs. Laying occurs at intervals over the course of a few days, each egg being deposited about two days apart. By far the most

Incubation, on average, lasts 35 days. The egg laid first will hatch first, so that in a clutch of three, it is possible for the last-hatched to be a week younger than its oldest sibling. Both the male and female develop an incubation patch on their lower breast that they nuzzle against the eggs. Because this patch is rich in blood vessels and is lacking some feathers, body heat from the parent can be more efficiently transferred to the eggs.

Diligence is the key word to describe incubating bald eagles. For only about two percent of the day are the eggs unattended by one of the persistent pair. Before a brief departure, the parent will cover them with a layer of grass or moss to provide insulation and to hide them from predators. During the long course of the incubating day, the sitting parent will rise about once an hour to carefully rotate the eggs and fluff the nest material. This helps to insure that the embryo doesn't stick to the shell, which would be fatal, and to contribute to uniform warming.

Incubation can become an endurance test for the adults, forcing them to sit unmoving while being pelted by rain, snow, and wind. The nastier the weather, the less likely that either stoic parent will leave the eggs unattended for even a minute or two. Inevitably, these long hours wear upon the incubating bird, and it will call to its partner and ask for relief. When exchanging these duties, both birds ball up their feet and step carefully around the eggs. Once in position, the bird taking over incubation lowers itself gradually onto the eggs with a gentle rocking motion. Once settled in, the adult then uses its bill to mound nest material around itself and the eggs.

Because both parents take part in the incubation process, each feeds itself during its off hours, unlike most other raptors where the female does all the incubating and must be fed by the male. Still, the female bald eagle does from two thirds to three fourths of the incubating.

Sometimes during this stage a wind storm may dislodge the nest, or flatten the nest tree, or a predator may steal the eggs. If such a disaster strikes early in the incubation, some pairs will lay a second clutch. The later in the incubation stage that the loss occurs, the less the pair is inclined to try laying a new clutch, perhaps sensing that insufficient time remains to prepare a brood for migration. During incubation bald eagles are particularly sensitive to disturbance, especially by humans, and may desert the nest or stay away long enough for the eggs to die. Some eggs are lost to raiding gulls, ravens, crows, raccoons and even black bears, but since the eggs are rarely left alone, and the parent birds are large and imposing, such casualties are rare.

There are other reasons for losses, though. Not all eggs are fertile. Some may be exposed too long to cold. Occasionally adults step on and break an egg. For these reasons, brood size and clutch size do sometimes differ. The odds are about equal that a successful pair will produce one eaglet or two. Survival of eggs to hatching can vary widely based on location, environmental factors, and human influence. On average, it appears that about 75 percent of those eggs laid will hatch.

Before the banning of the pesticide DDT, reproductive failure occurred in many parts of the bald

eagle's range due to egg shell thinning. Fortunately for us and the eagle, it is a long-lived bird with a long reproductive life. Once DDT was banned, and people focused on protecting the bald eagle and its habitat, those surviving pairs began the species' slow recovery.

Had bald eagles evolved a reproductive strategy similar to their favorite prey, fish, they likely would have disappeared completely except in the most pristine areas of North America. Fish live short lives, and scatter numerous eggs in the hope that one or two will survive to reproduce. Often, long before these offspring mature, the parents are dead. If this were the eagle's reproductive nature, adults would have perished long before the end of the use of DDT, and with almost no successful reproduction, the species could have come to an unnatural end.

HATCHLINGS

It seems a bit unfair that such a defenseless little thing as an eagle hatchling has to work so hard to enter the world. It can take up to two days for the chick to struggle from its egg.

The chick's work begins with its first cries from within the egg, signifying that its tiny lungs have begun to work. Although it first survives on oxygen stored in the egg's air chamber, very soon a hole must be opened in the shell to provide a fresh air source. Like most birds, the hatchling comes equipped with a bony projection on its beak known as an egg tooth. Using this tool, the chick punctures (or "pips") an air hole in the shell. The parents, hearing the chick, prepare for its arrival by sending out one or the other to hunt for food.

With a nearly constant peeping, the wee eaglet wriggles around in its shell and chisels away with the egg tooth. Apparently this is a tiring experience, for the chick struggles in five minute intervals over a 24-hour period. Finally, after long hours when it has pipped a ring around the entire shell, the bird wriggles free, about 35 days after its egg was laid. The adults are mere bystanders throughout the event, and do not assist the eaglet even if it becomes stuck.

Wet and pathetic looking at first, it only takes about four hours for the hatchling to turn from a soggy mass with closed eyes to a bright-eyed eaglet. Once dried, the eaglet's first coat is one of fluffy, pale gray down with a white patch at the throat. Though someday its powerful legs will be yellow, at first they are useless and bright pink. Wobbling on top of a long, thin neck sits a head that seems a size too large, sporting a beak that for now is dark gray, tipped in white. Within a day it will use that bill to peck at morsels of food offered to it by the anxious parents.

This rather peculiar looking little eagle, weighing about three ounces, will spend most of its first day sleeping and awaiting the arrival of any siblings. Because the adults begin incubation with the laying of the first egg, and because any subsequent eggs were laid at intervals, siblings will arrive in the order in which their eggs were laid. This staggered hatching can dramatically affect the development of the hatchlings, especially the last to arrive.

NESTLINGS

After the energetic brood has arrived, the parents tend to them ardently. Since the little ones are unable to regulate their body temperature, one or the other adult will spend long hours snuggled against them, a behavior known as brooding. For the first week or two, the gawky nestlings are rarely left alone. During the warmest part of the day, parents use their outstretched wings or bodies to provide shade for the susceptible offspring. During the cool of the night, nestlings will gather in a tight knot to share the warm breast of a parent. When the nights are particularly chilly, perhaps even a coverlet of grass will be pulled up around them by the caring parent. This night brooding continues for up to a month. Both adults and chicks sleep soundly through the night.

By now the eaglets have determined a pecking order, based on size and accompanied with much squabbling. Since the first hatched will always be larger because of the time advantage, it will dominate any other chicks in the nest. Antagonistic behavior between siblings peaks during this period, and it is during this time that deaths from competition occur.

About an equal number of males and females are born, but the order in which they are born can be significant. Although as adults, female bald eagles are always larger than the males of their latitude, male nestlings are initially larger upon hatching, and they also develop more quickly. Thus, if the first to hatch is a male, it will not only have the size advantage of first arrival, it will also be larger because of his sex. Because the largest nestling dominates any others, and because it is favored by the parents during feeding, it can sometimes cause the death of a sibling. Generally, these fratricidal deaths are not intentional or caused by an actual attack, but are due to starvation caused by competition. Most often these deaths occur in male-first, female-second broods.

If the clutch has two eaglets of the same sex, the only size advantage then is that of age, and fratricide is less likely. In order to avoid the male-first induced fratricide in broods of mixed sex, bald eagles have seemingly evolved a sex bias, so that females usually hatch first. If this is true, as research seems to suggest, the sex bias might occur at conception, which seems a truly eloquent example of evolution selecting qualities that lead to survival. Whatever the make-up of the brood, if an eaglet can survive its first month, the worry of fratricide is largely behind it.

Though the dominance of one nestling sounds distressing to us, it really serves some vital functions. First, fratricide is probably a means by which eagles adjust their reproduction to the food source. If food were unusually abundant, even the second or third chick would likely get something to eat. But this is not the norm. Even when there is enough food to share, the dominant nestling often keeps the less competitive sibling(s) from obtaining any.

When food is scarce, only that chick that protests the most, and elbows its way up to the dinner table, will get food. In fact, the parents selectively feed this nestling, and ignore the plight of any others, programmed through ages of evolution to insure that

the most aggressive nestling survives. These same aggressive qualities will be valuable later in life. And so the law of survival begins almost at birth for eagles. More typically, there is food enough for the average brood of two. The parents first feed the belligerent firstborn, and then turn to feed the other eaglet(s).

It is during the next few months that the food resources of a pair's range are taxed, for the demanding brood requires abundant food to fuel their spectacular growth. Unlike most raptors where the female broods while the male hunts, bald eagles share both duties, although males do tend to most of the providing. Throughout the summer, fish or other food will need to be delivered to the nest an average of about once every three hours, a schedule that might test the best hunter's abilities. Once the food is brought to the nest, the female will feed the nestlings and herself, although occasionally the male will tend to the whole of the feeding ritual.

It seems as though the nestlings are constantly hungry, and they are not bashful about announcing it. They scream, squeal and cry at their parents to induce feeding. It is the center of their lives. The parent very gently offers tiny bits with its beak to the anxious offspring. When sharing feeding duties, the female may tend one eaglet while the male feeds the other. Sometimes the male tears up and offers food to the female, who feeds it to the little ones. More frequently the female dominates the procedure, and may not even allow the male to eat any of the catch. It is no wonder then, given the female's intolerance for his presence during some feeding sessions, that the male bald eagle takes to eating a portion of each kill before delivering it.

Fueled by the regular deliveries of fish, the eaglets will grow to nearly two pounds by the end of their second week of life. At about two weeks of age they are capable of thermoregulation, although southern bald eagles still need the shading provided by adults. Heat stress can cause severe dehydration when the little eagles loose important body moisture as they pant to cool themselves. During the days just before and after the anniversary of their third week of life, the chicks will add nearly four ounces of weight per day! Until now they have done little more than eat and sleep, but presently they begin to wobble up to examine their world.

They take on the look of Dr. Seuss-like characters: round, bulging tummies and heads with odd bits of down sprouting. Their second coat of downy insulation has grown, one that is darker gray and woollier than the natal down it replaced.

As they continue to grow, eaglets get more demanding. While younger, they audibly demanded to be fed. But with their fourth week of life they begin to make the job of parenting a test of patience. No longer satisfied merely to ask to be fed, they begin to grab at a parent's beak or to jostle the adult in an attempt to get at the food. Little birds with enormous appetites, they gulp down giant chunks of fish, gorging themselves and filling their crops. At this stage they eat nearly as much as their parents, perhaps as much as two pounds per meal.

By the sixth week the youngsters will attempt to feed themselves from the carcasses delivered to the nest. At eight weeks they are proficient at moving

about the nest, and seem to practice striking at things with their feet, a skill they'll need to develop fully to fend for themselves.

Growing larger and more coordinated, the eaglets begin to tend more to themselves, and will spend long sessions preening their feathers, removing old growth and smoothing the new. Some of their earliest movements around the nest are prompted by defecation. Moving to the edge of the nest, they turn their back to the world and project their feces into space in a practice known as slicing. They also start to engage each other in play, romping about the nest, playing tug-of-war with bits of food or nest materials, and generally just frolicking. The frequent early squabbles for supremacy between siblings are gradually replaced with this play, especially as the size difference of any survivors begins to diminish.

By 60 days the eaglets have put on tremendous weight and have grown to nearly adult size. Their gray down coat, which first bleaches and then falls out, is now almost entirely replaced with dark brown juvenile feathers. Although they now look much like the majestic eagle they will become, they are still entirely dependent on their parents to provide food for one very important reason; they still are unable to fly.

FLEDGLINGS

As proficient a predator as the bald eagle is, it comes equipped only with the tools, not the knowledge. Animals with very short life spans rely heavily on instinct. But bald eagles are long lived birds, and while inherited traits certainly play an important role in a young eagle's development, much of its proficiency will need to be learned.

Pouncing in the nest, and playing tug-of-war with siblings begin the process. But these skills are useless until the eagle masters its greatest asset: flight.

A couple weeks of intense activity around the nest precedes fledging (first flight). The eaglets' feathers are nearly fully grown and they are nearly adult size. Sensing their abilities, the birds begin to jump above the nest, sometimes hovering over it in a breeze. Males will be more active than the females, but both sexes propel themselves with much flapping from one end of the huge nest to the other. They begin to use these wing-assisted hops to reach perching branches above the nest, expanding their world beyond the nest for the first time.

This isn't without risk, and occasionally an eaglet will fall to earth. While this tumble isn't generally fatal, surviving on the ground until it is able to fly can be perilous. If it falls into water, the eaglet may be forced to learn to swim days before it learns to fly. Once on land, an eaglet is faced with avoiding predators until it is ready to fly. Even then, it can be difficult to find an opening in the dense underbrush that will allow take-off. Though they wouldn't starve in the few days remaining until first flight, most fallen eaglets are fed by their parents.

At this late stage of eaglet development, the parents spend less and less time at the nest, choosing to perch nearby. This is probably a wise move, since the eaglets can be tough on their parents, charging them in mock attack or wrestling food from them. Because juvenile eagles actually have different

body proportions than adults, they are at least as large as their parents, and female juveniles now may be bigger than their fathers. With all the flapping and hopping about going on, the nest is no longer a friendly place for the weary parents.

Though I admit it is anthropomorphic, it seems that the first flight of an eagle must be a great thrill. To have the world beneath your wings, to discover this amazing ability within yourself, must give even an eagle an elevated heart rate! One could also assume that a little apprehension is the norm, especially when the fledgling discovers that it is easier to fly than to stop.

Males usually fly first, but the average age for both sexes is around 80 days. The fledgling's first flight can be either impressive or awkward, depending on the individual. Most fledglings find that they can glide well, and quickly discover how to flap to gain altitude. Landings are awkward for nearly every beginner, often ending in spectacular crashes especially when first attempting to perch.

As they practice their flying skills, the fledglings still depend on their parents for food, although feedings may take place away from the nest at perches. The young are still very aggressive about these meals, but they gradually begin to master a few scavenging skills and start to feed on their own. Shorelines are important to these young eagles, and while riding the prevailing winds, they begin to travel greater distances along the water's edge. During the first month after fledging, they tend to remain within their parent's nesting territory.

A great learning period ensues as the young eagles master scavenging and hunting. Now about 20 weeks old, the juveniles have been flying for over two months and are nearly self-sufficient. Their journeys back to the nest and their parents diminish. Flying skills are nearly mastered. They no longer require food from their parents, and the migration looms on the horizon. Birds from the north face the journey south, and young southern eagles may decide to move north to avoid summer heat.

After an intense and busy breeding season, the parents are again on their own. The cycle of reproduction is complete. Family ties cease. On the average, of the 75 percent of the eggs that survived to hatching, 85 percent of those nestlings lived to fly.

Now begins the most perilous year of the juvenile's life. Information on this stage of development is imperfect. Some results suggest as few as 10 percent of juveniles survive to adulthood, while others suggest survival may be as high as 50 percent.

For young and old eagles alike, the summer has been a busy one. In the few short months since their arrival at the nest site, the adult pair has built a nest, laid eggs and diligently cared for a brood of demanding chicks. Neither weather nor hunger has caused them to stray from their purpose.

No less wonderful has been the development of the young. The eagles of Wednesday Bay, and eagles all across their range, had succeeded in replicating themselves. In their company we saw the large brown juveniles, their offspring.

As the summer closes and the first chill northern nights hint of autumn, bald eagles of all ages enjoy a

brief respite. It is a time of feeding and recharging for the adults, and a period of exploration and learning for the massive young. All who are wise make the most of this break. For whether the eagle is a juvenile or adult, the most difficult time of the year awaits: the perils of migration and winter.

AMAZING DEVELOPMENT

It takes an amazingly short time, about 112 days, for an eagle egg to become a flight-ready juvenile. The following chronology is based on averages from around the bald eagle's range:

Incubation
- *35 days to hatching*
- *weight is three ounces at hatching*

Two weeks old
- *weigh two pounds, adding four ounces per day*
- *can begin to regulate own body temperature*
- *second, darker, woollier coat of down replaces natal down*

Four weeks old
- *begin to move about, jostling each other and parents*
- *eaglets can consume two pounds per meal*

Six weeks old
- *begin to feed themselves from food brought to the nest by parents*
- *size differential between siblings diminishes*
- *active play between siblings increases*

Eight weeks old
- *attain nearly adult size*
- *down replaced by feathers*
- *play, such as pouncing, mimics hunting skills*
- *begin to test wings by jumping, hovering, and hopping to nearby perching branches*

Eleven weeks
- *first flight occurs.*

CHAPTER SEVEN

WINGING IT THROUGH WINTER

. . . .

*I*t was the day before Thanksgiving. From our house on the hills above Lake Superior I could see dark waves march frigidly toward the west, hurried along by a steady wind. New snow lay thickly on the ground, but the wind that churned the lake had blown away the clouds that had laid it down, leaving a bright morning with brilliant blue skies.

Snug in our home, some months after our ranger duties had ended, we prepared for the family gathering we would host. I stared sullenly out the window, feeling a bit trapped after months in the wilderness, looking longingly at the wildness of the largest of all lakes.

I caught a movement high in the east, and as I watched, the object became a large, dark bird. Riding the strong wind it came quickly toward the house. Soon I could see the white of its splendid head reflecting the November sun. A bald eagle!

I had forgotten about the pairs that nested in our ranger territory, but the sight of this bird brought it all quickly back. As the summer waned we had watched juveniles from two nests learn to ride the thermals, watched in wonder at their great size and rapid development. The dark young of the year seemed to appear almost overnight, and indeed, in one sense they had. Tethered to the earth no longer, with the sudden discovery of flight they explored their territory and ours, and where only white-headed adults were to be seen

before, their large brown offspring appeared. By the time we paddled out of the Boundary Waters and back to civilization, the youngsters were well on their way toward fending for themselves.

Here, on this wind, as lakes froze and winter grasped the land, this beautiful adult floated past my window. I watched for long minutes as it gracefully responded to the air currents, traveling a mile in my view without so much as flapping once.

Then it was gone from my sight, west toward the end of the big lake where it likely would turn south to find the St. Croix River and eventually the Mississippi. Was it one of our own? Unlikely. But I liked the thought that perhaps it was, and that we and it had taken the same path south in preparation for the winter.

The wildness that it brought to my day was most welcome. I turned to the housecleaning with new vigor. By the time I was done it was entirely possible that our visiting eagle had traveled far on that wind, and was perched in the company of other eagles along the banks of the Mississippi River.

∽

MIGRATION AND ITS TIMING

Though there are some populations of bald eagles that do not migrate, most commonly those that live in the deep south or along coastal areas favored by temperate winds, all those that nest in regions where winter deals a frigid hand must flee before its rigors.

While the mated pairs toil to raise their young, large numbers of nonbreeding birds keep their own schedule. Unmated adults and subadults roam the hinterlands, feeding and wandering, perhaps even looking for mates or territories they can some-day call their own. But as the frost-fired leaves of autumn drift down from the trees, all bald eagles in northern climes must at their own time and pace drift to the south. By October, bald eagle migration reaches its peak.

It is a strange thing, this eagle migration. We don't commonly think of these birds of prey as migrators, at least not in the same sense we do geese. They don't depart in huge flocks, each bird a part of a uniform pattern, with families largely traveling in unison. Mated bald eagle pairs may not even migrate together, nor leave their nesting territory simultaneously. While most waterfowl leave in response to inclement weather, the bald eagle's departure isn't nearly as predictable, and some birds will remain in their home range as long as it is physically possible. The youngsters, having only just learned to fly weeks before, migrate alone, without the benefit of their parent's knowledge of routes or survival. Nor do bald eagles travel on

highly predictable sky paths as do waterfowl. Some drift great distances east and west with the vagaries of the wind, despite their generally southerly movement.

Such autumn migrations are tied to the availability of food: when winter denies access, the birds will move on. Because of this, autumn migration is in contrast to that of spring, which is likely related to the length of the day (known as photoperiod), which triggers the hormonal response to reproduce. In autumn, eagle travel is somewhat leisurely, with many stops to take advantage of food. Spring requires a more direct approach. Eagles fly greater distances each day and at a more rapid pace, intent on an early start to nesting.

ROUTES AND WEATHER

Some populations do not migrate, such as those in Florida, Arizona, and Louisiana, although as we've seen, juveniles of southeastern U.S. origin do migrate north at times in response to summer heat. If weather and food allow, many eagles choose to stay near their nesting territory, or to travel only short distances. Some bald eagles of the Pacific Northwest, for instance, travel only short distances, perhaps from inland areas where winter weather can grow severe, to the somewhat temperate shores of the Pacific and its abundant food.

While the severity of weather, and, therefore, lack of food, may spur departure, wind plays the most important role during bald eagle migration. Thermals are more abundant in the spring as the earth begins to warm, propelling these big birds with a minimum of effort. During autumn the cooling earth produces fewer thermals, so the migrating bald eagles take advantage of upwelling air along coasts, mountain ranges, and riverways. Those eagles that pass by our house ride such updrafts, using air currents generated by massive Lake Superior that are funneled down its precipitous north shore.

Far from a sign of laziness, this adaptation allows the bald eagle to travel long distances with a low expenditure of energy. Flying by flapping simply requires too much energy, energy that would need to be replaced through frequent feeding.

Like waterfowl, which follow predictable flyways and travel corridors well documented by scientists, bald eagles also make use of certain flyways, although they adhere to them much less rigidly. In the East, eagles from northern states and Canada follow a route between the coast and the eastern slope of the Appalachian Mountains. The Mississippi River and its tributaries provide migration corridors in the midwestern portion of the continent. Many northern eagles nesting in the central Canadian provinces follow paths through the plains states, making use of rivers and waterfowl refuges for feeding stops. This central flyway is bordered on the west by the Rocky mountains. From the far north of Canada, down through Alberta come bald eagles that migrate and winter in the intermountain regions. Bald eagles that nest west of parts of the Rocky, Cascade, and Sierra Nevada mountains follow the Pacific flyway, usually down the seacoast and salmon spawning tributaries.

Though their chosen flyways provide updrafts, eagles must still feed, and especially in the autumn their routes lead to known food sources. Juveniles wander much more than adults, for they lack the knowledge of what lies ahead. Migration, with the insecurities of food, the vagaries of weather, and the dangers of power lines and other obstacles previously unknown to them, is dangerous and often fatal for the young eagles. Until they have mastered migration, they live in peril, and this first year will be the most dangerous of their lives.

Adults seemingly know their way, and although they may be blown astray (or choose to travel along a new path), they have the knowledge and skills to survive the rigors of migration. Bald eagles traditionally congregate during the migration at areas of special food abundance, such as salmon streams. The adults taking advantage of these feeding opportunities may have visited these spots often over their lifetime, while the juveniles joining them probably stumbled across the opportunity. Young eagles in the company of adults at migration stops or wintering grounds are thought to learn of feeding opportunities by observing and mimicking their elders. The wise young ones will catalog the information for future use.

During each day of a bald eagle's journey it will resume migrating around 10 A.M., perhaps to take advantage of any thermals created as the day warms. By early afternoon it will stop to feed, although if food isn't present, the bird may travel for several days without it. After feeding the eagle may loaf about the feeding area, or travel on briefly, but by dusk it will have select-ed a roost for the night. If the hunting or fishing is good, an eagle may choose to stay for some time, otherwise the schedule will be repeated until it finds a spot to stay for the winter.

Often these wintering spots are no farther south than necessary. If we had the gift of flight, you and I might continue until we found greater warmth. But bald eagles have adapted to a certain amount of cold. Flying far-ther south would only mean a greater expenditure of energy, and a longer flight back to the nesting grounds.

WINTER FEEDING

Though there are several factors that influence where bald eagles spend the winter, by far the most important element is food. Cold weath-er and short days make life more diffi-cult for these magnificent predators, and these two conditions require that bald eagles carefully select their win-tering spot.

Because bald eagles do not hunt at night, and because cold weather requires a greater expenditure of ener-gy to survive, food must be abundant and easily obtained. Short days limit the amount of time that can be spent foraging. Cold weather puts more demand on the bird's ability to regulate its temperature, which taxes its energy stores. Bald eagles have responded to these environmental stresses by evolv-ing to limit the amount of effort entailed in keeping warm and flying to find food. To do otherwise would probably invoke the law of diminishing returns. In other words, eagles forced to forage widely probably couldn't eat enough to replace the amount of energy used to find the food.

This being the case, wintering bald eagles tend to utilize highly concentrated food sources. Carrion is a common entree, since a winter-killed elk or cow will provide many days of feeding during which the eagle will need to move only minimally. Similarly, spawning runs of salmon provide abundant food, and since the runs move up the river to the eagle, it can roost and feed repeatedly without much travel. Dams on many rivers in the central and midwestern parts of the country, provide similar feeding opportunities. Eagles feed on fish injured or killed passing over spillways or through turbines. Adept at locating such spots, bald eagles utilize the full potential of such winter habitat.

Researchers have documented the critical nature of these concentrated food sources to the point that they can almost predict the number of birds that will congregate at specific locations.

An eagle must consume between six percent and eleven percent of its body weight each day to survive. The colder the weather, the more it must eat. But as the weather cools, it must also restrict its energy expenditure. Hence it depends on foraging areas where food can be readily obtained.

Bald eagles try to minimize the time spent hunting or fishing. Under average winter conditions as little as one percent of the bird's day is occupied by these activities. The remainder of the bald eagle's time is spent loafing during the day, or roosting during the night, allowing an efficient conservation of energy.

Not that it always works that way. Occasional food shortages, such as the failing of a spawning run of fish or unusually severe weather, can com-

pel bald eagles to change their ways. They may be forced to fly and soar more to forage more widely. Sometimes they have to switch to less desirable or nutritious food sources, and have even been known to appear at garbage dumps. Because winter always is more demanding than summer even under the best of conditions, eagle mortality is highest during this season, especially among immature birds.

THE GREGARIOUS EAGLE

Though winter may be difficult for these normally reclusive birds, it also provides the opportunity for social interaction. Beyond foraging, the importance of such large congregations is open to speculation, but the benefits must overshadow the disadvantages or it would not occur.

Spats over roosting spots or tidbits of food seem almost to be expected of a predator that rarely gathers in more than pairs. Even families on the nesting grounds rarely gather together except while the young are mere nestlings.

A case may be made that eagles recruit mates during this period, for at no other time of the year is there such an availability of members of the opposite sex. Courtship-type displays are seen among wintering eagles.

Without doubt, juveniles still unskilled at hunting benefit from these aggregations, following adults to food. Many of them are for the first time encountering a world that has been greatly influenced by people. Associating with wiser adult birds may ease this introduction. And most

probably, the gathering of eagles increases the odds of finding food for the group. When eagles set out from their night roost in separate directions, more territory can be covered simultaneously in the search for food. Bald eagles, with their tremendous visual acuity, have the amazing ability to spot their cohorts tens of miles away as they soar. Even if an individual doesn't see where others drop down to feed, since they will share a common roost come evening, it can follow the knowledgeable birds to the food source the next morning.

ROOSTING TOGETHER

It is probably this last behavior as much as any that explains why bald eagles share roost sites, although other functions are certain.

Since the bald eagle really is a sound sleeper, communal roosts could serve as protection, since the larger the number of eyes and ears, the smaller the chance of being surprised by a predator, although bald eagles face few true dangers from other animals.

With nearly 70 percent of their 24-hour, winter day spent in a communal roost, some important sexual purpose may be served as pairs select each other or renew bonds.

There may even be a thermal factor involved. Roosts are sometimes located in particularly well-protected sites or dense coniferous trees. Eagles may gather because the roost is the warmest spot, and perhaps they benefit from each other's radiant body heat.

Despite the test of winter, bald eagles do expend energy on activities that are not clearly related to hunting. Occassionally they soar together in large, swirling masses, known as kettles, perhaps for the pure joy of riding on a thermal. At other times, mass bathings occur, and as one eagle takes a dip it seemingly infects the others with the desire for a chilly dunking.

Communal roosts can be noisy places as the birds establish a hierarchy. Old or aggressive birds will vie for the favored, highest, nighttime branches. As one eagle enters a roost and displaces another, a sort of domino effect may be precipitated as each displaced bird moves down the line to oust yet another, amid vocal squabbling. These dusk gatherings and arguments finally give way to the dark, sleepy night, and not until sunrise will most birds depart to feed.

As the days lengthen and the world warms again, the bald eagle feels within itself the urge to depart. Hormones and daylight trigger this urge. Eventually these wintering places, once filled with the vociferous squabblings of eagles, will grow silent as each bird leaves on its long flight back to its home range.

Spring migration will take less time than the one that brought them south. Fewer places to feed, better thermals to carry them farther each day, and the biological clock that ticks toward reproduction all reminds them not to dawdle.

Many eagles have died over the winter, a sad but inevitable occurrence for all that swim, crawl, walk, or fly. But the promise of a new generation of these spectacular white-headed predators is carried in the urges and the genes of every adult that has survived to reproduce. Perhaps the newly mature have found a mate during the gregarious winter months and will for

the first time find a place that they can call their own. Lanky juveniles will set out to discover the adventure that is life, wandering and learning and dying.

Winter has ended. The lushness of life flows forth. Ever masterful, the bald eagles of North America set out to fill the land with beauty, fierceness and grace.

TO SEE AN EAGLE

Those who wish to see a bald eagle can do no better than to look for them at migration stops or wintering areas. The following is a partial list of such places.

Tennessee
- *Reelfoot Lake hosts many wintering bald eagles beginning in late autumn.*

Missouri
- *Swan Lake National Wildlife Refuge attracts numerous bald eagles that feed on waterfowl during the winter.*

Mississippi River
- *From Minneapolis/St. Paul through Illinois, residents of the Midwest can watch wintering bald eagles at numerous places on the Mississippi River. Contact the U.S. Fish & Wildlife Service or state conservation departments for specific recommendations.*

South Dakota
- *Bald eagles winter along the Missouri River at refuges such at Karl Mundt National Wildlife Refuge.*

Rocky Mountains
- *Wintering populations of bald eagles gather near rivers, especially in Glacier, Yellowstone, and Grand Teton National Parks, also in Colorado's San Luis Valley.*

Utah
- *Both Cedar and Rush valleys play host to wintering bald eagles from December through March.*

Alaska
- *As many as 3,000 bald eagles gather in autumn at the Chilkat River Bald Eagle Preserve.*

Washington
- *Look for eagles along the beaches of Olympic National Park, at Nooksack River, and at the Skagit River Bald Eagle Natural Area.*

California
- *Check near the Oregon border near Tule Lake, Klamath Lake, and Bear Valley National Wildlife Refuges.*

East of the Mississippi River
- *Bald eagles are more easily seen here at dense nesting territories. Florida's Everglades and Chesapeake Bay both have large populations.*

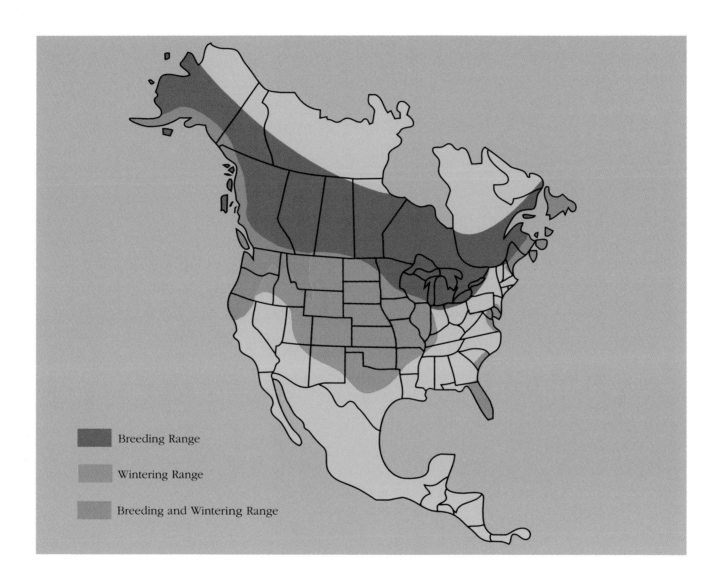

Breeding Range

Wintering Range

Breeding and Wintering Range

CHAPTER EIGHT

EAGLES IN OUR WORLD

We have not been kind to the bald eagle. Since western civilization set foot on this continent, bald eagle populations have declined throughout much of its range. We have made what was once a world in which humans and eagles largely co-existed, into one that we consider "our world," in which other species must adapt or disappear.

Unfortunately, it is highly unlikely that humans and eagles can coexist even under the best of conditions without some adverse effects for the birds. The bald eagle's penchant for remote locations and its dependence on waterways puts it in direct conflict with our development of these resources. Our best efforts will only serve to maintain a healthy eagle population on the fringes of our own, and we will never again see the abundance of eagles that was the bounty of the virgin continent. Still, great strides have been taken in recent decades to insure that the bald eagle survives in those places where habitat still exists. Bald eagles are now being seen in places where they were absent for many years, and the short term picture looks bright. Only time will tell if this situation will be sustainable considering current human population trends.

With the coming of the first people over the land bridge from Asia, humans on this continent have always caused eagle mortality. That eagles flourished anyway speaks to the fact that the population of Native Americans was not large, and that the philosophy of these first immigrants is based on respect for all living creatures. Native Americans also utilized natural resources in a far different manner than does western civilization, and although they may have, at times, competed with bald eagles for resources or space, their system did not rely on altering natural landscapes, which left the eagle's habitat intact.

The reverence that Native Americans hold for the eagle and other living things does not extend to the point where they consider it wrong to kill, which stands in direct contrast to the current animal rights dogma. But in taking animals, so that they might eat or use these creatures for ceremonial purposes, Native Americans sought a balance, much as they observed among wild creatures themselves. The killing of an eagle was highly ritualized and probably rare.

Many tribes killed eagles for feathers and bones, which served important cultural and ceremonial purposes. Most of the more publicized methods of capturing eagles relied upon the use of meat or fish as bait, while the hunter hid beneath or near it. The technique used by the Lakota serves as an example of how other plains tribes hunted eagles. Hunters would dig a pit on a high ridge frequented by the big birds. A row of poles covered with skins supported a layer of turf and other camouflage. After ritual preparations and a purifying sweat bath, the hunter would crawl into the trap and, placing a rabbit lure above him near a small opening, await the arrival of an eagle. If the hunter was fortunate, an eagle would take the bait. At that instant the tribesman would reach through the hole, grab the eagle by its legs, and draw it into the pit where he would wring its neck. The eagle was then ceremoniously placed on a nest of sage prepared for this event.

In the Pacific Northwest, Bella Coola natives would erect a blind near a river frequented by bald eagles. From his hiding place the hunter watched the bait of salmon he had placed on the riverbank. When an eagle arrived the hunter used a long pole to lower a noose over the bird's head.

The Eagle Cult of the Hopi tribe captured young eagles from nests. These birds would be fed and kept alive until fully grown. At the Niman ceremony the eagle would be killed during a ritual prayer offering. After removing the valuable feathers, the Hopi respectfully buried the eagle remains in a special eagle cemetery.

These killings certainly had some small impact on eagle populations, but they paled in contrast to what was about to come. Native Americans, and aboriginal people around the globe generally tend to take only that which the local bioregion can easily provide. Europeans, wherever they colonized, tried to remake the land in an image of their home. The resulting importation of non-native plants and animals forced them to remove native competitive species. Native Americans did not fear that competition the eagle or any other predator would deny them a share of the over 60 plus million bison

that roamed the west. The new Americans, once they slaughtered the bison to make room for livestock and grain, set about removing all predators that might eat their cattle and sheep. Both golden and bald eagles made that hit list.

THE POPULATION DECLINES

Until we very recently began to change our ways, we waged full-scale attack on bald eagles on this continent. We did it both intentionally and by accident.

At first, we affected eagles mostly through displacement. Humans and bald eagles prefer much the same habitat. As much as they need river, lake, and ocean shorelines for nesting and hunting, we seek these too, for needs as varied as home sites and commerce. As we began to consume the forest wealth of this land, we furthered the bird's decline as we turned actual or potential nest trees into ship masts and cities.

We also viewed the eagle as a direct competitor, and killed them indiscriminately as vermin. Though eagles rarely attack livestock, we took as evidence that they did the sight of eagles feeding on cows or sheep that had died of other causes. Our animosity grew, and persists in some places today, until we bountied this magnificent bird or employed men to trap, poison, or shoot them.

Nowhere did we kill larger numbers of bald eagles than we did in the American west and Alaska. As cattle and sheep replaced bison and elk, we attempted to rid our rangelands of predators, avian and otherwise.

Though we directed much of this rancor toward the golden eagle, significant numbers of bald eagles fell to our wrath. We shot them, caught them in leg hold traps as they settled in on bait set for wolves and coyotes, and killed them with poison-laced carcasses. And this slaughter was not a thing of our distant past. We've killed many eagles during this century, and in some places it continues today.

For instance, during the 1930s some California sheep growers killed eagles by the hundreds each winter. Not to be outdone, some Texans followed suit, killing thousands of eagles through the decade of the 1940s. Many were shot from pursuit airplanes.

From 1917 through 1952 Alaska offered an eagle bounty and rewarded those who turned in dead bald eagles. By the time the program ended, some 128,000 eagles were turned in for reward. Those that were wounded, or killed but unretrieved, probably numbered in the tens of thousands. Many of these early eagle eradication programs were either funded by state and federal governments, or carried out directly by their employees.

As recently as the 1970s in Texas and Wyoming some ranchers set out again to rid their lands of eagles. Though by then the birds were protected by law, extensive poaching took place, often again by air, with several hundred eagles killed. Unfortunately, eagle poaching continues today, though those who partake have switched to more clandestine operations. Much of the killing is done with poisoned carcasses and takes place on remote ranch lands. Documenting these abuses is difficult. Great amounts of money have been

spent by the U.S. Fish and Wildlife Service to pursue eagle killing cases, and the return for that money and effort has been meager.

Unfortunately, admiration of, and interest in, Native American lore has become more of a burden than a blessing for the bald eagle. Americans and Europeans, enamored with the ways of the first Americans, have created through this infatuation a demand for Indian artifacts. Since many of these artifacts contain eagle parts, particularly feathers, a black market has arisen. Native Americans are partially exempted from eagle protection laws so that they can continue to possess eagle parts for religious purposes. Unfortunately, this legitimate use has served as a shield for Indian and non-Indian poachers. The confusion inherent in discriminating between feathers legally obtained and those taken by poachers has allowed the greedy to supply the black market with eagle parts. The U.S. Fish and Wildlife Service penetrated two such black market rings during the 1980s. In Washington state 60 eagles were known to have been killed; in South Dakota as many as 300.

Finally, we continue to kill eagles for no particular reason, not even one of greed. Though no one knows for sure, based on those cases discovered, it is thought that hundreds of eagles are killed each year by people who simply use them for target practice.

THE CHEMICAL THREAT

There is no doubt that the chemical revolution we've experienced in the last century has spawned many benefits for humans. Our lives are easier, our food more abundant, our lifespan longer. While we reaped those benefits, we sometimes were poisoning the earth.

The bald eagle's decline during the middle of this century was one early and dramatic example of us using too much of a good thing. When we discovered just how beneficial a little pesticide may be, we decided that a lot would be even better. It is an example of how shortsighted we can be, and of how one individual can make a dramatic difference.

While we spread DDT across the landscape, a retired Canadian banker and proficient amateur ornithologist was watching the eagles at his winter home in Florida. Charles Broley was a pioneer of eagle research who in baggy pants and with a fiery curiosity set about to band the eagles along the Gulf Coast. Beginning in 1939, he surveyed this region of Florida. By 1946 he had identified 140 active nests that produced 150 eaglets, on which he placed leg bands after perilous climbs into their lofty homes. We are very fortunate his curiosity drove him to this endeavor, for within just a few short years of his first banding, the bottom dropped out of eagle reproduction. Without his initial bandings of what had been a healthy Florida eagle population, little base line data would have existed.

In 1947 Broley noticed the first decline, but nothing could have prepared him for what he would discover in 1952. In all his wanderings that year he could locate only 11 active nests, which produced only 15 eaglets. Not that the adults had disappeared, mind

you. They were still around. They just couldn't reproduce.

That this coincided with the rapid spread of the use of DDT during and after the war years didn't escape Broley. He postulated not only that the decline of bald eagles and the rapid rise in use of DDT was more than just a coincidence, but that DDT was the cause. The battle to save bald eagles didn't end when this theory became known, it only began. Broley also demonstrated that eagles in his Ontario homeland were suffering similar fates. Soon, confirmations of similar reproductive failures elsewhere were documented, not only of the bald eagle, but of other raptors.

Eventually the link between DDT and these nest failures was made. This substance, spread on both crops and forest to control insects, had been washing into the surrounding aquatic environment. As each creature consumes another, it inherits the load of DDT or other pollutants stored within. This process, known as biomagnification, results in increased accumulations of toxins in those creatures farthest up the food chain. The bald eagle's reliance on fish caused them to ingest large quantities of the poison. A few eagles that received massive doses died outright, but most affected eagles exhibited an inability to reproduce. It was finally proven that even low quantities of DDT inhibited calcium metabolism in the female bald eagle. Insufficient calcium caused the birds to lay eggs far too fragile to withstand incubation.

Industry fought the ban on DDT, and governments responded slowly. Not until 1970 in Canada, and 1972 in America, was a ban on DDT legislated.

By this time the bald eagle populations in the United States outside Alaska had become locally extinct or were dangerously near that status. Some Canadian eagle populations faced similar reductions.

Once DDT was banned, eagles still suffered from its effects as ecosystems took time to cleanse themselves. For instance, survival was low in Maine until managers provided a clean source of food during the winter months, setting out numerous contaminant-free carcasses for eagles to feed upon.

Another insidious threat surfaced in the form of lead poisoning. Bald eagles frequently consume waterfowl, which may have ingested the spent lead pellets of shotgun shells, and, therefore, eagles consume some of this lead themselves. Lead consumption is sometimes fatal to waterfowl and eagles alike. After lengthy litigation and research, the use of shotgun shells containing lead for the hunting of waterfowl was banned in America in the late 1980s, largely removing this threat.

More recently, reproductive failures and deformed eaglets have been discovered in those bald eagles nesting along the shores of the Great Lakes. The cause is linked to toxins such as polychlorinated biphenyls (PCBs) found once again in fish. Mercury emitted from incinerators and industrial plants has also been finding its way into fish stocks across the continent, deposited as it falls trapped in rain and snow. Many states and provinces now issue fish consumption guidelines for humans, but eagles and other creatures that similarly depend on this food source can't voluntarily limit their intake. Mercury has been linked to reproductive failures and severe nerve

"I cannot live without books"

Thomas Jefferson

damage in many species, and can be fatal even to adult humans. In Minnesota, even lakes within the Boundary Waters Canoe Area Wilderness, far from any direct source of mercury, are recording a three percent to five percent increase in mercury per year. Even if mercury doesn't impair the reproduction of bald eagles, it may severely limit the reproductive success of those fish on which it preys. Acid rain poses another threat. Acid deposition kills all aquatic life within a lake, which would include eagle foods.

In the Pacific Northwest, salmon stocks have been seriously diminished through a combination of habitat destruction (logging in riparian zones and the construction of dams) and overfishing. Although fisheries managers have supplemented natural salmon stocks with hatchery fish, this is of little value to bald eagles since the fish most often return to the hatchery. In a natural state, salmon spawning takes place out in the open where they can be preyed upon by eagles, or can be scavenged once they die. Similar prey base changes have occurred elsewhere, and the affects of these on bald eagles are only now becoming understood.

Of increasing concern is the continued development of shorelines. With each year, more and more people choose to build cottages or homes on lakes. Previously inaccessible lakes are being reached by new roads, even in the more remote sections of Canada. Research has clearly shown that the higher the human density on a lake, the lower the eagle population. We compete with them for space, we encroach on their need for solitude, and heavy human fishing pressure can lower fish stocks to the point where the resource can support fewer eagles.

We know one thing for sure. As an indicator species of the health of the environment, the bald eagle, unfortunately for it, serves the purpose well. Located as far up the food chain as we are, inevitably what occurs to the bald eagle will happen to humans as well. If for no other reason than that rather practical one, bald eagles deserve our observation and protection.

STEWARDS OF BALD EAGLES

Congress passed the Endangered Species Act in 1966, providing a tool to further bald eagle protection. The bald eagle was listed as Endangered in 1967 in all contiguous states except Minnesota, Wisconsin, Michigan, Washington, and Oregon, where it received Threatened status. With this listing, attempts began in earnest to rejuvenate the bald eagle population. Great research efforts were expended to understand this bird and its needs, and the resulting information provided natural resource managers a means of enhancing eagle habitat and reproduction. The bald eagle has responded well to management efforts. In some regions its population seems secure enough to change it from Endangered to Threatened status. Some of this improvement has come from removing toxins such as DDT from the environment. But much of the good news is due to the efforts of researchers and managers alike.

Bald eagle management is more intricate than we suspected. We learned, for instance, that more than just the eagle's nest tree needed protection.

Much of this work was carried on in the Chippewa National Forest in Minnesota, resulting in strategies that ultimately suggested a succession of zones around the nest site. Each zone sets limits on human use within, with a "no trespass" area nearest the nest tree and progressively less retrictive zones farther away. In more recent years, the shape of these zones, which were once concentric circles, has changed to represent the needs of the birds based on where they nest, perch, and hunt. As useful as this information is, it is effective only when applied, which generally only occurs on public lands where resource agencies can exert control. Eagles, however, are unaware of these imaginary political boundaries.

During the low ebb in bald eagle production after the ban of DDT, some excellent efforts, such as those in New York state, were made to reintroduce eagles to areas from which they had disappeared. Most reintroductions used hatchlings or fertile eggs gathered from healthy eagle populations in places like Minnesota, Canada and Alaska. Using a technique called "hacking" borrowed from falconers, eaglets are raised in cages located in natural habitat. Being careful to remain as unobtrusive as possible, human caretakers guard and provide food to the young eagles. Eventually, they are released into the wild. Food is provided for a time until the young eagles can fend for themselves. Since the first bald eagle hacking program in 1976, New York has enjoyed encouraging natural reproduction from these released birds.

Researchers have shown that wintering habitat may be the most important cog in the machine of bald eagle management. Most eagles still nest in regions of the north where people have yet to dramatically change the landscape. But winter habitat is often in regions already heavily developed, limiting the bald eagle's opportunities. In some cases we've unintentionally created winter habitat by establishing waterfowl refuges or building dams that create open water and fish kills.

But besides a reliable source of contaminant-free food, bald eagles need secure winter roost sites and places to hunt that are free of human activity. As we've seen, winter is a naturally stressful time for eagles, and any additional stress in the form of diminished food stocks or interruptions of resting and hunting can further put them in peril. Consequently, protection from human activities and development within critical wintering areas is essential. Whether it is identifying and protecting those natural winter sites that still exist, or enhancing those we've quite accidentally created, attention is turning to the needs of eagles in the difficult months of winter.

TO LIVE WITH EAGLES

We are fortunate that we learned enough about the bald eagle to help its resurgence. Today, we see eagles in places where just a few decades ago they were rare or extirpated. We bought its salvation at huge expense. Great stores of money have gone into the necessary research and management schemes that aided these efforts, most of it paid by a willing public.

As we continue to search for ways to help the bald eagle, we must remember that it is not enough to

secure nesting habitat, or clean foods, or winter roosts. Each of these things needs to be present in the proper balance. While food may be the bottom line for the survival of an individual bald eagle, having undisturbed access to food when stressed by winter becomes nearly as important, for an eagle unable to feed is just as dead as one that can find nothing to eat. Similarly, tall trees on prime waterfront are not enough to insure adequate reproduction if competition with people for food, or disturbance during nesting makes the nesting site of little use.

In the end, we must realize that the bald eagle has an admirable range of survival skills and adaptations, the result of millions of years of evolution. In many ways, it is an adaptable creature, and because of that, it has fared well across a broad range. Think of the eons through which it has survived. Remember that it soared almost everywhere across this continent, changing, adapting, living its life in varied habitats. There is nothing we can teach an eagle about survival.

Remember, as you look at these wonderful photographs or pause to watch an eagle soar, that like most creatures that have had a brush with extinction, the bald eagle just needs a place and the resources to fulfill its biological destiny. That is all it really asks of us. In the short run we can provide for its needs, and its admirable skills will take care of the rest.

We have proven that we, too, are a most adaptable race. Our challenge now, should we decide that saving our fellow creatures from extinction is one that is important, is to find our own balance with nature.

Perhaps that is the greatest lesson we can learn from studying bald eagles. It has evolved a reproductive strategy that tends toward stability and avoids over-exploitation of resources. Though they may compete with, or prey on, those neighboring creatures, a balance is found within the large ebb and flow of population growth and decline.

We know that the bald eagle is more ancient than we. Is it possible that in this manner it is more highly evolved?

PROTECTING THE NESTS

Did you know that bald eagle nest trees are protected? Whether they are located on federal, state, or private lands, it is illegal to destroy a nesting tree. This protection extends also to the birds, their eggs, and their nestlings. Bald eagles may not be harassed or otherwise driven from their nests. Most nests on public lands have some type of zoning that regulates human activity within the vicinity. However, this management strategy is not mandatory on private lands.

THE LEGAL EAGLE

Many events and laws have led to the demise and recovery of the bald eagle. A short history follows:

1782 - *The bald eagle is declared the symbol of the United States of America.*

1917 - *Alaska passes a bounty on bald eagles. Repealed in 1927.*

1940 - *The Bald and Golden Eagle Protection Act is passed by the Congress of the United States, stipulating a penalty of one year imprisonment and/or a $5,000 fine for the taking, possession, or commerce of eagles except for certain exempted circumstances.*

1966 - *Passage of the original Endangered Species Act.*

1967 - *Except for Minnesota, Wisconsin, Michigan, Washington, and Oregon the bald eagle is listed as Endangered in the contiguous United States.*

1972 - *DDT is banned in the United States.*

1973 - *The Endangered Species Act is amended, providing increased protection for the bald eagle and directing funds toward research, habitat acquisition, and management.*

1978 - *The Endangered Species Act is amended again. The bald eagle is listed as Threatened in the five previously exempted states while remaining as Endangered in all other contiguous states.*

1990 - *U.S. Fish and Wildlife Service considers reclassifying the bald eagle as Threatened, rather than Endangered, due to increases in the bird's population.*